Seasons of Grace

Seasons of Grace

The Life-Giving Practice
of Gratitude

Alan Jones
John O'Neil

with Diana Landau

John Wiley & Sons, Inc.

Published by John Wiley & Sons, Inc., Hoboken, New Jersey

Published simultaneously in Canada

For general information about our other products and services, please contact our Customer Care Department within the United States at (800) 762-2974, outside the United States at (317) 572-3993, or fax (317) 572-4002.

Wiley also publishes its books in a variety of electronic formats. Some content that appears in print may not be available in electronic books.

Library of Congress Cataloging-in-Publication Data:
Jones, Alan W., 1940–
Seasons of grace : the life-giving practice of gratitude / Alan Jones, John O'Neil.
p. cm.
ISBN 0-471-20832-9
1. Gratitude. I. O'Neil, John R. II. Title.
BJ1533.G8 J66 2003
179'.9—dc21   2002014028

Printed in the United States of America

10 9 8 7 6 5 4 3 2 1

For Cricket
—A. J.

For Patricia
—J. O.

The authors gratefully acknowledge the following copyright holders
for permission to quote from:

Letters to a Young Poet by Rainer Maria Rilke with the permission of
Random House, Inc.

Every Eye Beholds You: A World Treasury of Prayer, copyright © 1998 by
Thomas J. Craughwell, reprinted by permission of Harcourt, Inc.

"Clocks Cannot Tell Our Time of Day (No Time)," copyright © 1941
by W.H. Auden, from *W.H. Auden: The Collected Poems* by W.H.
Auden. Used by permission of Random House, Inc.

Dream Work, copyright © 1986 by Mary Oliver, used by permission of
Grove/Atlantic, Inc. and the author.

Contents

PART III
Autumn: The Grateful Self

PART IV
Winter: Living into Gratitude

Acknowledgments

In full knowledge that we slight many who could be mentioned by name, we wish to thank the following in particular:

First, we are grateful for the steady support of our respective families. Alan's wife, Cricket, and John's, Patricia, have put up with our whining, long meetings, and countless hours of unavailability. For their special contributions to the book's content we are also thankful. Our children and grandchildren offer us constant reminders of why we wrote about gratitude.

Second, to Diana Landau, who patiently knit together our diverse approaches, we owe whatever symmetry and order the book has. We are thankful for her subtle but firm creative nudges and for the contributions of her colleague, Nancy Friedman.

Third, special appreciation to our book therapists (posing as agents), Muriel Nellis and Jane Roberts, and for the brilliant editing of Tom Miller, who was able to see the whole of it.

Finally, to Meghan, Ellen, and Katherine, who support us every day in countless ways, our great appreciation. And to all those who shared stories and offered critical comments, profound thanks.

Introduction

Gratitude and "Going Live"

Gratitude is not only the greatest of virtues, but the parent of all
the others.

—CICERO

In 1993 a mutual friend told each of us, Alan and John, "There's
someone you should meet." This kind of urging tends to provoke
anxiety because, as with a blind date, the two people meeting may have
less in common than their friend imagined, may even dislike each other
on sight. Nonetheless, we agreed to have lunch and learned—in the
course of two hours at Alan's neighborhood Japanese restaurant—that
we shared not only strong threads of experience but also a bent for
self-examination and seeking sources of renewal in our lives. We're so
inclined partly by temperament and partly by virtue of what we do for
a living.

We both "work with people" and between us encounter a wide
range of them, from varied circumstances and with vastly varied goals,
drives, responsibilities, and responses to life. Alan, in his ministry at
Grace Cathedral, talks to people who profess faith (apparently
unshakable) in God's goodness and purpose in the world, and just as
many perennial spiritual questioners. He comforts those in despair,
prods the complacent to action, urges the virtues of stewardship on
the wealthy, and represents his church in dialogue with other religious
traditions. He has specialized in bringing together the insights of the
spiritual and psychological traditions.

1

John, in his work as adviser to corporate leaders, typically encounters people deeply immersed in the universe of management, organizational structures, and strategic planning. Often they are people whose personal lives and development are shoved into the background while they take care of business. But personal issues nearly always emerge in the course of dealing with the problem at hand. John focuses on helping them figure out what they want out of life and to understand more fully the mystery and pitfalls of "success"—why does success so often fail to deliver what it promises?

During that first meeting, we discovered that while we operate in different spheres and use different vocabularies, we are both dealing with choices people have to make about how to be in the world. Some choices lead to a kind of living death, others to "going live." And not long after meeting, we had the chance to see some of those choices in action, in a way that strengthened our bond and moved our friendship forward, while jointly leading a seminar at the Aspen Institute.

Since then we have co-taught many times, leading discussions, workshops, and seminars mostly on organizational and leadership renewal. Our audiences have ranged from members of the Young Presidents Organization to Silicon Valley venture capitalists to wealthy families seeking ways to avoid "affluenza."

We've found that to do our work well—individually and together—we must look past the outward accomplishments, accouterments, or problems of people and their organizations. From Alan's parishioners and church leaders to John's stressed CEOs, they have more in common than separates them.

All live and work and raise families in a culture that is changing at light speed and that, through the mighty media, imposes standards and encourages strivings that doom even the most successful to failure on some level. It is a culture that promotes the virtual at the expense of what is real, depriving us of what historian Andrew Delbanco calls a "sustaining narrative." And virtual living elicits, in response to any search for larger meaning, flimsily packaged answers that ignore shades of gray, promise solace without struggle, and offer safe identities at the expense of commonality. Striving for perfection and control becomes a setup for disappointment, relieved only by the short-lived comfort of accumulating stuff.

In our work together, we've come to focus on developing and using a practice of gratitude. One discovery that has emerged is how effectively gratitude can work to release us from the mindless and devastating stress built by habit into our daily lives. The first step on this path is recognizing that gratitude isn't just an exercise of etiquette: one more virtue we should cultivate, one more damn thing to do. Rather, it is our spontaneous response when we wake up to the fact that life is a gift, and our sense of wonder is restored.

In the interest of full disclosure, we confess that we struggle with these issues as much as the people who seek our help. So we began to think about how we ourselves could insinuate—into our already bursting schedules—practices of wakefulness leading to gratitude in its largest sense. Could we find support, a community of like-spirited people? We wondered why some seem to have more capacity for gratitude than others. And we wanted to discover, through personal stories, how people actually practice gratitude.

We are two men who have reason to be grateful. We are friends who come from contrasting backgrounds and are old enough for regret and alive enough to be expectant. We have made mistakes and made wrong choices. But we also made a decision to say yes rather than no to life. This may sound pretty simple-minded, but we know a lot of people who are unaware of their basic response to life. Bringing our responses from the depths up to awareness is one of the ways we experienced change in our own lives.

Both of us discern a spiritual crisis—and opportunity—in the modern world. We know that just because you have a reason to be grateful doesn't mean that you actually feel gratitude. Some people, with every reason to be thankful, live their lives resentfully, ignoring the evidence in front of them.

We offer this book as a way to gather and present what we have learned, separately and together, about practicing gratitude: from our own lives, our friends, and our work. And we hope it may serve to guide others to pay attention, learn gratitude and joy, and embrace being a little subversive.

George's Story

George is a good friend of ours who's had more than his share of life's hell, especially in recent years. Prostate cancer nearly killed him, and he lives alone in a rundown part of town. His wife died a few years ago; he has a couple of kids who keep in touch regularly but live half a country away. A practicing if not devout Catholic while he was married, he admits that his faith has pretty much slipped away. What puzzles all of George's friends is that he is always so inexplicably cheerful—and in a way that doesn't make you feel uncomfortable. There's nothing forced about his upbeat spirit.

When we asked George to share his secret, he said there are basically only three responses to life: "Damn!", "Help!", and "Thank you!" He'd tried them all. The first one he described as "like pouring all your energy down a rat hole." The second was appropriate more often than he would like. But it was the third that produced the most mileage. "I faced a lot of crap in my life, including death, and I decided I might as well live, and live as gratefully as I could. Every day's a gift and I don't want to waste it in either cynicism or self pity."

George went on to describe a small ritual that he's made part of his daily life: "I am struck by the simple fact that my day goes better when I begin it by pausing for a moment to let myself feel astonished. I wonder that there is a day at all, that there is a me to live it. I am amazed that there is anything at all, that there is a me at all—even a depressed and faithless me. And if I'm lucky, this sense of amazement is sustained by gratitude."

We want to take George's advice and explore the gratitude response. We are convinced that gratefulness is the *primary* response to the gift of life, though we'll have to look at the other two from time to time. Sometimes we have to work our way through "Damn!" and "Help!" before getting to gratitude, and it's often a struggle to get to that grateful place when life is hard and unfair.

We're not claiming that gratitude is always easy. In the face of tragedy and evil, it is the hardest spiritual practice of all.

George showed us that gratitude is a stance towards life. The word comes from the Latin *grata* or *gratia (given, gift)*, from which we get our word "grace." It suggests a cycle of giving and receiving. Think of the way Italians are always saying *Grazie!* Grace! Thank you! And think how awful it is to be designated *persona non grata*. How should we translate that? It means a person who has been banished from a group or who is denied access to the community. Beneath this, perhaps, is the idea of someone who has no sense of gratitude, no thankful appreciation of the gift of life?

In this book we are going to chart and calendar what we call "seasons of grace"—occasions and opportunities for gratitude and appreciation, without which no one is fully alive. Some of them may come as a surprise.

Gratitude is a practice that develops over a lifetime. This practice involves a journey through stages, in which gratitude finds countless forms of expression.

We hope that it will become clear as this book progresses that the practice of gratitude is one from which other blessings flow.

Going Live

George's story, and many others, show gratitude acting as an antidote to the feeling of being disconnected. Every occasion for gratefulness is in some way a recognition that we belong to the world and to our fellow beings, that we exist in the community. Practicing gratitude can restore us to our rightful place in the world. Then the world becomes something shared, not something to exploit. It begins to recover its sacred character—the "sacred" being simply a way of referring to the really real.

We use the phrase "going live" to describe an experience when life in all its fullness and fragility breaks upon our consciousness, when the here and now is as exciting as it gets. Real-time performance with all its inherent risks and rewards. Knowing what an awesome thing it is to be alive and aware. (The alternative is "going dead"—an insidious process that can happen almost without our noticing as we pursue our busy lives, and that distorts and impoverishes our vision of life.)

It's easy to feel grateful for life's gifts when the circumstances are just right: at times of personal triumph, in the exhilaration of momentous events like births and weddings, on trips and vacations planned for maximum thrills or inspiring surroundings. At such times, the shot of ecstasy that is going live is expected. But does it always come?

You've got to be alive to the possibility that gratitude can spring out from the darkest corners, that you can receive from someone who may seem to have nothing to give, or that the gift may come disguised. Even scarier, that gratitude could turn your life upside-down, force you to eliminate the half-realized dreams, the delayed hopes, the running rationalizations that may get you through the night. It could compel you to embrace mortality in a way that gives you joy, or to laugh because you are not in control.

If you are engaged in a practice of gratitude, you don't need to wait for "special" moments. (In fact, they often let us down!) By practicing gratitude, we can hope to go live at any moment, however ordinary, at any time of the year. How about today, or tomorrow? How about spring? Just a few weeks ago, as of this writing, the winter solstice came and went; the days began to get longer. In the colder regions, life lies waiting underground, under snow. In Mediterranean climes like our California home, buds are already swelling.

How about now? How about this morning's exercise class, this afternoon's phone call with the sales rep you like, the billboard that makes you grin on the drive home, tonight's story time with the kid? The sting of cold wind on your face, the sudden memory of a lost loved one, the healing rest of bed? Will these, and a million other facts of your life, come to you as burdens that exhaust and deplete you, or as gifts that strengthen and inspire? Practicing gratitude can make the difference.

Seasons of Grace

This book gathers material for the practice of gratitude from many sources: our own lives, stories from friends and co-workers and clients, observations and readings from wise folk in many fields. In thinking about how to weave it all together, we tried to identify the dynamics of how a practice of gratitude grows and develops. Our four-part organization took shape as a kind of soul's journey through progressive stages:

1. Awakening to the sources of gratitude in our lives
2. Exploring and nurturing them

3. Using a practice of gratitude to go live, to grow into an authentic and resilient self
4. Learning to live gratefully in relationship with the world—and giving back to the world

Awakening. Exploring. Growing. Responding. Each of the four parts, or stages, is linked with a season. First, Spring, the time of rebirth, generation, the ground opening and softening to receive rain and begin growth. Here we take the first step in developing any practice of gratitude: to open, or reopen, oneself to experiencing wonder and amazement. We awake to wonder at everything that is. So much has been given to us through no doing of our own. It should elicit amazement.

None of us has lost our capacity for wonder completely; in part, it's what enables us simply to get up in the morning. But all can benefit vastly from sharpening this sense because a deepening practice of gratitude is built on it.

We will try to locate the *sources* of gratitude in our lives—what gives rise to gratefulness. An example from Spring: if we're grateful for sheer existence, we need also to notice and thank the earth and its resources, our parents and other guides and mentors, the gift of health and healers, and (for those of us who are spiritually inclined) a generous Creator. We talk about the wonders of nature in this part, about seasonal cleaning of our spirit's house, and "grateful sweat"—the cleansing mercies of hard work.

The next stage is Summer, when we move from amazement and attentiveness to actively seeking out, exploring, and cultivating occasions for gratitude. This is not only the grateful heart's flowering and maturing, it is also a time to take stock and face our fears. In Summer we consider and celebrate the realms of sensory and aesthetic pleasure: the body and its beauty, recreation and rest, the making of gardens, the gifts artists bring us. A special gratitude can grow from watching the fully alive play of children or even emulating them in the carefree climate of summer.

In the third part, Autumn, we can begin to harvest the fruit of earlier seasons. Through a deepening gratitude practice we gain self-understanding. In the light of gratitude we can go live more often.

Autumn chapters describe the gifts of growing into an authentic life, how we locate and nurture the stories that shape our lives and lead us into gratitude. And other kinds of experience that help us go live: feeding the mind, meaningful journeys, and spiritual pursuits. We also discuss occasions for gratitude in our work and avocations.

Finally, in Winter, we envision the grateful self going into the world, multiplying and strengthening our connections with others. Here we explore themes of intimacy and community, meanings of the hearth and the feast, the symbiotic work of generosity and gratitude in a fully human life. Winter leads us to look at how we celebrate our closest bonds through food and conversation. We glimpse the role of gratitude in repairing a world torn apart by misunderstanding and malice. And, as the year draws to a close, we (like our distant ancestors) contemplate our own endings and the need to let go of all earthly joys.

In Winter, we face the challenge of being thankful for our inevitable deaths and, by implication, for all the human ills associated with our mortality. Side by side with celebrating light, laughter, and life's bounty we must also learn to cherish the difficult, dark, messy parts, the destiny we all face and the heartbreaks along the way.

Going live makes us vulnerable by pointing out uncomfortable truths like our need for each other and the fact that we are going to die. It means that struggle and darkness are *normal* parts of human experience, as are choosing new possibilities and taking risks. This is where gratitude is difficult, often manifesting as tears to the eyes and a sense of the fragility and precariousness of life. We wake up and think, "How could I have been so blind, so stupid!" It's the place where laughing and crying converge, a dangerous kind of gratitude—where we need to laugh until it hurts.

By using the seasons as an organizing device we don't mean to suggest that the stages of a gratitude practice unfold in a neat, orderly march, like the lengthening and shortening days or the waxing and waning moons. Our deep cultural familiarity with seasonal phenomena makes them a useful image, and specific practices or rituals might best be pursued at certain times of the year. But we never graduate from the need to wonder and marvel, and so always remain in the spring of our practice. Autumn's work of self-recognition continues all our lives, and winter is always around the corner, even at the height of summer's bloom.

Methods to Our Madness

In addition to our own thoughts on going live through gratitude, we offer the stories of people, real and fictional, who often speak more powerfully than we can. The reader will meet some people for whom gratitude is a delightful, daily practice, like a spring garden in full bloom. Other stories are of high achievers for whom success became life-threatening, their striving an addiction, cynicism and fear the windows through which they viewed life.

Each chapter also will bring opportunities to locate what's not working in your own life and to enrich your gratitude work with active practices. These may be meditations, exercises, prayers, interactions, celebrations, or physical activities; some can be practiced at home, some at work or while traveling, and so on. Developing rituals that are meaningful to you is a keystone of any spiritual practice. It asks you to devote time and thought to an activity whose explicit aim is spirit-nurturing. In most cases, these rituals also bring pleasure. But granting yourself the luxury of planning and carrying them out can be very hard amid life's urgent (or supposedly urgent) demands.

Rituals that bring us into gratitude help revive our capacity to make merry and to dream. We are creatures who not only work and think but sing and dance, tell stories and wait before mystery. We also know that our survival entails our capacity to *change*—but to do that we may need mechanisms that undermine our routine. Change can come, for example, by way of celebration. Mindful, personal rituals can honor or interpret the past, and open up the future.

Our spirits long for a bigger world to play in than the tiny cosmos of routine and work. We also need the kind of rejoicing that isn't frivolous or sentimental—that recognizes life is sometimes tragic and that even tragedies can be a powerful generator of gratitude. A sense of the tragic and the ridiculous is part of the fullness of celebration. We weep. We laugh. We give thanks. And our guide to the pathways of gratitude could be *anything*.

PART I

Spring

Opening to Wonder

Our friend Gracie was digging up and dividing fire lily bulbs early one northern California spring—that is, a warm day in February. The tall, fast-spreading plants had nearly taken over her tiny, sloping backyard; it was time to clear some of them out. Moving to a new spot, she plunged her trowel into the crusted soil and worked it around the edge of a big clump of tubers. She heard a muffled, sporadic buzzing noise but couldn't quite locate the source. She pried further, loosening the soil and pulling roots away from its grip.

The buzzing got louder and angrier, and suddenly, out of the dark hole, lurched a large bumblebee, staggering across the loose soil as if drunk and shaking dirt off its wings. After a few seconds, it launched itself unsteadily and slowly flew off, still buzzing in a low, sputtering, grumpy sort of way.

Grace was so startled she dropped her trowel and just stared after the creature, open-mouthed. "I felt like a god who'd just unearthed a bear from hibernation," she recalls. "I guess I've been gardening long enough to kind of take spring and rebirth for granted: you plant bulbs, they come up; the bare trees are suddenly covered in pink flowers one day, and all that. But this—having a living, moving, complaining creature emerge from under the ground after I don't know how long—just seemed miraculous. Thinking about it years later, I'm still gripped by awe. And I still laugh, remembering how annoyed that bee sounded."

There's something magical indeed about spring after the deadness of winter. Imagine a barren piece of earth. But look at it closely. Do you see a hint of greenness, the smallest and tenderest of green shoots? The human heart is like piece of dark earth; even when it may appear barren, it is always pregnant with imminent life and possibility. Spring is a time rich with symbols of growth, like germinating seeds, swelling buds, Easter eggs—the world is brought to life by an energy working in the dark that Hildegard of Bingen, a twelfth-century mystic, called *Viriditas,* the greening power of spirit. Its opposite is a deadening cynicism, a truly barren place where nothing can grow.

The poet George Herbert, after a period of spiritual deadness, wrote:

> Who would have thought my shrivel'd heart
> Could have recovered greenness? . . .

He, along with poets and mystics through the ages, found that dying and rising—moving from the death of winter to the newness of spring—is a principle of the inner life. A springtime rebirth of the spirit is available to all of us, and this rebirth is both the propagator and the fruit of gratitude. Practicing gratitude serves to continually renew our life force, like sun and water on the soil, and seeking springtime—looking for those tiny green shoots—is a primary exercise for stimulating gratefulness.

The first step on a path to practicing gratitude is noticing or rediscovering astonishment: developing the capacity to see with fresh eyes an infinite array of everyday wonders—like a bumblebee awakening and emerging from the ground, or any number of even more prosaic miracles. Being alive to the unexpected, joyful surprise. If we let the small wonders register and resonate, we can begin to see more and more of what surrounds us as sheer gift. Then gratitude flows with no prompting.

Sometimes it takes a real surprise to jolt us into noticing what we're so used to taking for granted, or to break out of the grip of winter. And sometimes the gift comes in disguise.

1

The Unexpected Gift

Love wholeheartedly, give thanks and praise—then you will
discover the fullness of your life.
　　　　　　　　　—Brother David Steindl-Rast

Risking Our Inner Lives

Sometimes we want to break out of our own skin—to smash through
the boundaries we sense are confining our spirits so we can experience
something like ecstasy, so we can feel alive. From all around us come
reports of people feeling dead, or at least distanced from the kind of
living they sense is possible. Feeling disconnected, unrooted, unreal.
Ordinary tonics—stimulants, sex, travel—don't seem to carry enough
charge to jolt them back to life. They demand stronger medicines.

We die by seconds and live by inches. As a matter of course, we
maneuver cars through heavy traffic at speeds where survival is a matter of good brakes and millimeters of tire tread. We take off and land in
planes (mostly safely) and undergo medical procedures of extraordinary complexity (not quite as safely). Yet most of the time, living at the
edge of literal death is not part of our awareness. We often push our
fears down and reduce them to something manageable. The little
near-deaths somehow help us feel more alive; some even seek ever
more hazardous pursuits to counter the fear of a living death.

"New economy" types, occasionally emerging from their self-
imposed work prisons, sign up for expensive adventure trips that involve
strenuous trekking, whitewater boating, or high-altitude ascents—

another kind of addiction to velocity. At the extreme, risk-takers throw themselves off precipices, bridges, and buildings; for them, even sky-diving has become too safe and predictable. Then there are the professional daredevils: athletes who put their bodies on the line for fame and gain, or journalists obsessively drawn to whatever world conflict is raging hottest.

That a few people are drawn to such extremes is surely part of the human behavior curve. But why, today, do so many find the need to amp up their already stressed lives? The answer, we think, is that they sense their *inner lives* are at risk. The risks we take with our inner lives are usually less obvious but more insidious—starting with simple neglect. Deprived of attention, the starving spirit weakens and soon can barely make its voice heard above the external din. Our most fundamental needs—for loving contact, communal reassurance, sensory stimulation, ritual, and ceremony (to name just a few)—may go unmet. And all the stock-market scores, trophy homes, partners, and toys disappear down a bottomless void. Unless we can feed our inner life, our ability to perceive and savor the outward world in all its splendor withers.

Your Gratitude Quotient

We need to develop a sense of smell to help us figure out where true life can be found. We may not lack courage, but we sometimes lack discrimination in our risk-taking. Not all risks are life-bearing.

Our hunger to break out and go live is a sign that we're on to something important. We're on the edge of a great adventure of the human spirit—if we only knew it. Somewhere inside, we know that our right destiny is to experience joy, warmth, sweetness, communion, cathartic sorrow, creative work, and play—not just to imagine or recall those feelings in fleeting moments, but to feel fully alive all the time. Spring. *The surest path to that ever-renewed sense of being alive is through grati-tude.* A grateful heart, we've concluded, is an absolute prerequisite to a fully human life.

Gratitude—as conviction, practice, and discipline—is an essential nutrient, a kind of spiritual amino acid for human growth, joy, and cre-ativity. Take away the daily experience and expression of gratitude, and life is quickly diminished. Like a weakened immune system, the spirit is left vulnerable to the diseases of cynicism, anger, low-grade depression, or at least an edgy sense of dissatisfaction. Gratitude-deprived, we suffer a relentless loss of vitality and delight.

It's easy not to notice when gratitude goes missing. More and more gets taken for granted. Privileges such as physical health, a child's love, freedom of action, and a comfortable home are all seen as entitlements. We fail to *notice* things. Travel becomes boring; even exotic adventures bring a very short wave of satisfaction. Meals are consumed mindlessly, without any ceremony of appreciation. Friends disappoint us. Boredom becomes a constant and finally sadness settles in, an unwanted, lingering guest. Under such conditions, there's no chance for the greening power of spring to take hold.

We want to expand your idea about what gratitude means. We're guessing that your gut response to the words "gratitude" or "being grateful" is slightly impatient or even dismissive. "Grateful" is what you feel when someone gives you a present, right? Or does you a favor? At least, it's how your parents *said* you should feel, and they trained you to say "thank you"—even for that ghastly sweater you got from an unpleasant aunt when you were seven. Later, expressing gratitude carried the weight of obligation. You were suddenly in someone's debt. You owed. This idea of gratitude carries the burden of having to pay back.

At best, gratitude can sound like an incredibly simple, harmless notion. "Live with a grateful heart? Sure, why not? Couldn't hurt. I'll do it! Check that off the list." But you might as well simply *decide* to live mindfully, upon first hearing of that fundamental principle of Buddhist thought. Mindfulness is being completely aware each and every present moment. Such life-changing, soul-shifting practices tend to be intellectually simple to grasp but elusive to master in everyday life. Incorporating them into our being takes not only the will to do so but time and effort.

So the practice of gratitude, as we conceive it, has a lot in common with living mindfully—in a heightened state of awareness—and our approach to it borrows from many spiritual traditions. In fact, all the great religious traditions emphasize wakefulness, gratitude, and compassion.

A deeper conception of gratitude encompasses a stance toward life and a discipline in which it is forged, tested, and strengthened. In this stance, we choose to be open to what life offers us: to seek out all that makes us fully alive and present to experience, to acquire discernment about what works toward that fullness of life in the long run. Ram Dass says that whatever happens in your life is your *curriculum*—the vehicle for your learning. In practicing gratitude, we *choose* to view life fundamentally as a source of joy, the world as loving and giving of what we need, rather than the reverse. Or, as the poet Wendell Berry wrote, "Be joyful even though you have considered all the facts."

Why does appreciation for the gift of life come more easily to some than to others, regardless of objective cause? This is one of life's great mysteries. Some who have been through horrendous circumstances are able to appreciate and enjoy life, while others blessed with abundant resources respond to life mainly with resentment, anxiety, or anger. The capacity for gratitude seems to have little or no relation to wealth or circumstances, or even to whether or not we were raised in a loving home. M. Scott Peck, in his book *In Search of Stones,* even speculates that some people carry a gene for gratitude that others lack.

We would agree that everyone seems to have some mysterious, built-in setting on the gratitude spectrum. To be congenitally inclined toward gratefulness is a great gift in itself, as Peck observes. Some might call it a gift from God; others would consider it a result of brain chemistry. It doesn't really matter, though. What matters is that everyone can benefit by nurturing this gift, to whatever extent we're endowed with it. And if you think your gratitude quotient is low, then deliberately cultivating a grateful heart can make that much more difference in your life. Whatever we're least good at, we need to practice most.

Opening to Wonder

Alan set down this memory when he began thinking about occasions in his life when he was surprised by an unexpected gift:

> A sunny afternoon in Paris a few years ago I took the Metro to Montmartre and walked up the steps to Sacre Coeur, when all of a sudden the world was ablaze with glory and the light of it was around me and in me and shining through everything. Where did this joy come from, with its gift of presence and rightness? What triggered it? Was

it the kid with the ice cream—great gobs of it dripping down her seraphic face? Was it the couple entwined on the grass who had eyes only for each other? Was it the sunlight playing on the leaves of the trees, delighting the eye with every shade of green imaginable? I don't know and I could drive myself crazy trying to work it out. All I do know is that it had something to do with amazement at the sheer gift of life.

It seemed to me then that joy is a bit like reading a story that never comes to an end. You get caught up in it—even lost in it. The joy of it is that it is all gift. I also had tears welling up. I discovered the strangeness of a joy because tears can be mixed up in it. You never know when life is going to surprise you and stun you with a joy that makes your eyes wet with tears.

Just for a few moments on that September afternoon, joy became my raison d'être. I knew why I was here. I learned something about adoration—the amazement at being our true selves in the presence of life as gift. Joy makes adoration, compassion, and community possible. And while these are possible, so are we. And it had something to do with very ordinary things like the kid with the ice cream, the lovers in the park, and all those greens of the leaves that luminescent afternoon on Montmartre. I learned that joy is in the particular, and I still worry a little bit about missing what's under my nose.

The groundwork of any gratitude practice is opening to wonder, recovering the ability to be astonished. In order to experience gratitude as more than a trivial acceptance of what is given (perhaps owed) to us, we must first be able to experience life's gifts as truly extraordinary and miraculous. In this way, the springtime of gratitude entails a revival and deepening of the imagination. Our horizons easily become narrowed, our perceptions blunted. The soil on which our growth as humans depends can be poisoned by patterns and strategies of denial, cynicism, resentment, and revenge.

Humans have an inexhaustible need for something that honors our capacity for wonder—we see this demonstrated over and over in scientific research and scholarly inquiry; in our awe of natural phenomena and our urge to explore space; in our admiration for humans who perform miraculous feats of creativity, virtuosity, or athleticism. We all need to get out of our skins, to journey outside the confines of our own little world. However, that need can also get us into trouble. If it's not fed something nourishing then it will attach itself to activities that can do harm, such as taking unreasonable risks and doing foolish or destructive things.

Risk taking exerts such a powerful attraction because it is related to freedom—the awesome freedom to break boundaries and go beyond our limits. That's why some of us tempt fate by risking all that we have and are. Like the dormant seed in the ground, we want to respond to the warm sun and the soft rain, break out of our shell and see the light of day.

Practicing gratitude both feeds our need for wonder and frames ways we can get out of ourselves (off the treadmill of me, me, me) and risk appropriately and courageously. We can then dare to love. We can risk openness to others and the world. We can be less attached to material things. We can see how absurd our mentality of scarcity is in the light of our relative wealth. In short, we can stop playing dead and become fully alive. Specific practices that help open us to wonder include slowing down, paying attention, giving up some control, and being alive to the unexpected.

Slow Down

To experience wonder, you have to notice what's going on around you, and most of the time our lives are going by in a blur. We need to cultivate a new attitude towards time if we are to open ourselves again to wonder and heart-piercing surprise. Slowing down is not an end in itself, but a first step toward a more creative and soul-nurturing relationship with time. Instead of being irritated or enraged by life's ordinary inconveniences—waiting for an elevator, sitting in traffic, even being stuck on the runway on a delayed flight—we can use them as opportunities to open up and take notice. Unsolicited gifts often come at these inconvenient moments.

Pay Attention

Every day the world offers itself to be seen. Seeing things with a grateful eye requires attentiveness and engages our imagination; imagination is a way we take part in the world, not escape from it. We can train

ourselves to see the immensity of the commonplace, the world offering itself to our imagination every moment. A poem, a piece of music,
a particular smell: if we pay attention, these can open up new worlds.

Such ordinary experiences not only affect the present moment but
also shape our sense of the future. In other words, they give substance
to hope. Sometimes it's as if a piece of music or a painting or a book
takes possession of us, and we feel amazed and honored to have such
guests inside us. We become the host of the undreamed and unexpected. The genuinely new becomes possible. Springtime returns.

Going live involves deciding where to focus our attention. Human
beings, suggests the poet and translator John Ciardi, "are what we do
with our attention." Or as the mystics would say, we are what we contemplate. If we give our best attention to things that ultimately fail to
satisfy us, we get into trouble. Going live, then, may be the act of
attending to what's really going on inside and around us. This can be
unnerving, because it sharpens our awareness of life's fragility and difficulty. But it also awakens us to life as a gift and starts the wheels of
gratitude turning. The positive feedback that gratitude produces is
what allows us to stay live, to not shut down.

Give Up Control

"Do something every day that won't compute," says our friend George.
Part of what he means is to get yourself out of the place where you feel
comfortable and in control in order to expose yourself to someplace
where you can't predict the outcome.

Technology's pervasive power offers the illusion that everything is
fixable. Worse yet, it can render life sterile. Putting ourselves in its
thrall is like paving a garden or putting down astroturf so that nothing
can grow: you have more control but the garden is gone. Our efforts to
make existence more manageable narrow our horizons; spring is effectively banished. If we wait to marshal all the facts and get everything
under control before engaging, we miss the game of life. Remember
Groucho Marx in *A Day at the Races*? His brother Chico convinces
him that he can't place his two-dollar bet until he has purchased a
breeder's guide and a whole slew of other pamphlets. By the time
Groucho has looked over all of them and been utterly confused, the
race is over.

Opportunities for giving up control come our way whether we choose them or not. Airline flights are a good example. It's interesting to observe how people choose to use this time. For some, work simply continues: keyboard out at wheels up. For others this time is spent reading a novel or watching the movie. On one flight to Australia from San Francisco, a neighboring passenger watched six movies back to back.

What if you used some of your flight time for practicing gratitude? The underlying premise of grateful flying is that you are out of control—if you arrive safely at your destination, someone else has made it happen. That reminder of how we depend on others is a binding element of gratitude practices.

Gratitude Practice: Flying

First, get comfortable and block out as many distractions as possible. Next, focus on the remarkable fact that you are *not in control*. This is a huge leap for many of us who go through life feeling bound to control mechanisms. For those who are used to holding positions of power and responsibility, such as doctors, business leaders, and parents, the idea of not controlling the environment and worrying about outcomes is virtually impossible. As a passenger on an airplane your only responsibility is to relax into the experience of *not* being in control.

Finally, do a simple mental inventory of all of the gifts you possess: family, friends, talents, privileges such as freedom, and so on. Savor each gift. Feel no requirement to be critical. Just enjoy thinking of those small moments you relish with a lover, a grandchild, or a treasured friend. This can be retrospective or prospective. It can be anything you wish to make it: a story of a time when you felt happy or exalted, a mental image of a favorite place with a special person.

The best thing about a flying gratitude practice is that it can be completely open-ended in intent. The result can be a deeply refreshing meditation—or a nap. You may arrive at your destination better prepared to enjoy your work or holiday. The outcome, like the flying, is not in your control. Enjoy!

DISCOVER THE UNEXPECTED GIFT

What is the movement of spring that draws life out of the seemingly dead earth and pushes us towards the light, toward going live? What needs to happen to plunge us into the twin mysteries of self-knowledge and interdependence—the signs of being fully alive? For one young woman, it happened suddenly.

Grace Happens

Rita is thirty-two, single, and, according to her former friends, moving down the ladder fast. Her immigrant family gave her a great education, and when she graduated from Smith, she went to New York to "make it"—and did for a few years, as a buyer for a big department store. Her world fell apart when she got pregnant. She felt caught between wanting the baby and not wanting to lose the life she had come to take for granted. At first she couldn't tell her parents, whose old-country Catholicism was still strong. She felt no support from her boyfriend. But in the end she decided that abortion, for her, was out of the question. She took her savings, returned to her parents' home in southern California, and had her baby, Miguel.

Much to her surprise and that of her career-minded friends, Rita's life wasn't ruined, it was restored. She slowed down and felt herself becoming more grounded and self-confident. She's the first to admit that this isn't the path for every woman in her situation. But as much as she appreciated her education and opportunities to succeed, she knew something had gone sour, that her promising life held little joy. Rita and Miguel are doing fine. Rita is back at work and in a relationship that seems, as she says, "to be going somewhere." She says she's never felt more alive. "My former friends often used to say, 'Shit happens!' Now I know that grace happens too."

Falling deeply in love is one way of falling into the springtime mysteries. People often receive an unexpected gift in the form of a wake-up call: an accident, a chance meeting, an illness. Something happens (a minor or major catastrophe) that invites us to get down to basics and think about what really matters—life and death, the possibility of being lost and the promise of being found. Sometimes it's something quite small—a letter we shouldn't have opened, the discovery of a lump in the breast or the groin while showering. Almost anything can place us on the edge of life, open doors we didn't know existed or would prefer to keep locked. By such events and discoveries we are embedded more deeply in the human community, which needs us more than we realize.

Hidden mercies crop up in ordinary life all the time. Karen is an avid and expert gardener; her backyard urban garden was a neatly sculpted masterpiece of clean-swept surfaces, carefully weeded borders, trimmed container shrubs, espaliered fruit trees, and gracefully draped arbors. As she gradually became disabled with severe arthritis, she fell into near despair; unable to pay a professional gardener, she had to watch as her meticulous handiwork grew untidy and overgrown.

But lately, she told us, her response has been changing. "I found that since I could only work for short periods, I had more time to just sit there and notice what was going on in the garden. I started to appreciate wild plants that I once would have ruthlessly yanked out, and things growing together in interesting patterns that I never would have planned. My cats had a new jungle playground, and there were more birds and butterflies than ever before. Best of all was what happened this spring: an old rosebush that had been on the property when we moved in had never bloomed, though I faithfully pruned it each year. This year I couldn't—and since March it's been producing the most gorgeous coral roses!"

By practicing gratitude even in the worst circumstances, we give our lives integrity. All the bits and pieces of our experiences are in touch with each other: the hurtful and the whole, the good and the bad. Spring, with its greening power, allows the seed to break open and struggle towards the light.

Gratitude Practice: Feeling Alive

Unexpected gifts don't always appear through the dark, of course. Try to think of those times when you have felt most keenly alive. Was it hearing your child's first cry? Beholding a grand view at a magic hour during a walk? Were you making love? Absorbing the shock of a family tragedy? Accepting an unexpected gift of praise? Inhaling a delicious fragrance like old roses or warm pie? When you find one or more such moments, focus on what you felt.

This is a kind of foundation practice for strengthening your gratitude quotient. Beneath the powerful—often fleeting—states of joy, terror, or passion, gratitude is germinating. And as we learn better how to cultivate gratitude, it begins to flavor all parts of our lives, expanding our souls and opening us to the perennial spring of wonder.

2

Singing Creation

To be grateful is to recognize the love of God in everything
He has given us. . . . Every breath we draw is a gift of His love,
every moment of existence is a grace. . . . Gratitude therefore takes
nothing for granted, is never unresponsive, is constantly awakening
to new wonder and praise. . . .

—THOMAS MERTON

A few years ago, Grace Cathedral in San Francisco hosted a celebration of indigenous peoples and their gifts to the rest of humankind. The church was temporarily turned into a rain forest—not with real rain, of course, but with the sounds of the forest. Chief Leonard George, of the First Nation People of British Columbia, spoke to the gathering about the purposes of tribal education, to which he was deeply committed. He was speaking, in particular, about the adolescents under his care. His task, as he saw it, was to help them appreciate and value themselves, so that when they got up in the morning and looked in the mirror they were able to love, delight in, and celebrate what they saw.

A defining trait of our species is our consciousness of existence—we know that we are alive and part of a wondrous creation. This consciousness has prompted awe, wonder, praise, and celebration in countless forms. It has made people ask, how did we get here and why are we here: questions that have been creatively pursued through myth, religion, and science. And throughout most of human experience there has been a recognition of existence as a gift, as the primary gift.

This recognition comes more easily for people who see creation as the work of a creator spirit or spirits, be it Yahweh or Krishna or the Great Mother. Grateful prayers and praise are central to every spiritual tradition. It's more challenging for those who cannot reconcile a world infused by spirit with a world subject to the laws of physics and bio-chemical explanations of life. But whether or not we are embedded in a spiritual practice, we must find ways to experience and express grati-tude for this most primary gift, or we become gratitude-impaired on every level—set adrift in creation, unrooted, lost.

Sacred Songlines

Among the ways indigenous peoples locate themselves—geographi-cally and psychologically, though they wouldn't make that distinc-tion—are drumming, music making, and storytelling. Oppressed and marginalized peoples often seem to be in touch with levels of experi-ence unfamiliar to the rest of us. Australian aboriginal myths, for example, speak across cultural lines about how a community of trust is maintained by stories, dreams, and songs.

In his novel *The Songlines,* Bruce Chatwin investigates how the aboriginal world is held together by songlines or dreaming-tracks. Cre-ation myths tell of legendary beings who wandered over the land in the Dreamtime, singing out the name of everything that crossed their path—birds, animals, plants, rocks, waterholes—thus singing the world into existence. They sang creation.

A character in the book, Arkady, explains:

Each Ancestor, while travelling through the country, was thought to have scattered a trail of words and musical notes along the line of his footprints, and . . . these Dreaming-tracks lay over the land as "ways" of communication between the most far-flung tribes. "A song," he said, "was both map and direction-finder. Providing you knew the song, you could always find your way across country. . . . In theory, at least, the whole of Australia could be read as a musical score."

"To them, the whole of bloody Australia is sacred," comments the Westerner, Chatwin's narrator. We might add, "The whole of the bloody world is sacred!" Each aboriginal child, according to the myth, is born with a fragment of the Song. The suggestion is that if we all remembered the music we were born with, we would not only be bound together in one community but we could move through the world at ease because we would know our way about. We would have at our fingertips the musical map, the songlines, crisscrossing our history and experience.

Human beings today, in contrast, are being asked to find our way around a world where the Golden Arches are the only recognizable landmarks. We of the developed nations have claimed the entire globe as our home territory, but at what price? How can we possibly sustain the kind of intimate relation to creation that aboriginal peoples have had? These are not easy questions, but if we are to celebrate creation and our place in it, we need some kind of shared music to guide us. Each generation needs to sing and tell their stories to keep the lines deep and clear.

There's a story about the "first" English poet, Caedmon (d. 680?), who thought of himself as an ungifted cowherd—until he found his voice. The story goes that Caedmon one night saw a heavenly visitor who commanded him to sing. But what should he sing about? he wondered. "Sing of what you know," said the wise being. "Sing of creation." And so he did. He joined the famous Abbey at Whitby and spent the rest of his life composing songs.

Each of us has something to sing about. We're not suggesting that everyone can be T. S. Eliot or Robert Frost. Not many of us are going to be up there with Placido Domingo and Frederika von Stade. But we do each have a unique voice to add to the symphony of creation. Is there a "you" locked away inside, of which you are only barely and occasionally aware? There are fragments of a greater song in you that need to see the light of day.

Construct the World Generously

The journey toward praising creation and our own place in it can begin with the smallest of epiphanies. Alan recalls standing in a supermarket checkout line where a mentally challenged young man was bagging groceries. A middle-aged woman, looking very worn out, had just finished paying for her order when she caught sight of the bagger and held him in her gaze. He looked up and beamed happily at her. She looked down briefly, then raised her head, pushed back her hair from her eyes and smiled back.

What had happened? For want of a better word, a small epiphany. The young man had become visible and valued in a special way. A human being, seen for who he or she is, is breathtakingly significant. Such experiences are available to us many times each day. They enable the heart to sing in gratitude.

Our view of the world as a generous and giving place—or the inverse—is shaped by many influences. If we are lucky, we have courageous and caring parents, teachers, and mentors who model this stance for us. And we will be schooled in ways that set our imagination free. Literature professor Martha Nussbaum, teaching a Dickens novel at the University of Chicago Law School, asked her students to speculate about why Dickens attached so much importance to nursery rhymes. She asked one student if he had ever sung "Twinkle, twinkle, little star/How I wonder what you are?" What did he think about when he sang it? Did he remember how it made him feel as a child? The student responded by recalling an image of

> a sky beautifully blazing with stars and bands of bright color. This wonderful sight somehow, he said, led him to look in a new way at his cocker spaniel. He would look into the dog's eyes and wonder what the dog was really feeling and thinking, and whether it might be feeling sadness. Now it seemed to him that it was right to wonder about the dog's experience, and to think of the dog as having both love for him and the capacity to feel pleasure and pain. . . . All this, he said, led to new ways of thinking about his parents and about other children.

Nussbaum wonders why a rhyming tune would lead a boy to imagine that the starry sky was benevolent rather than threatening, or to think of his dog as loving and good rather than devilish and cruel. Why bother about the dog's possible feelings in the first place? Why not take pleasure in an animal's pain? The nursery rhyme, she points out, nurtures a tender humanity within us and stirs up the prospect of friendship. It tells the child to imagine the star "like a diamond," rather than "as a missile of destruction, and also not like a machine good only for production and consumption."

The nursery rhyme nourishes a generous construction of the seen. Our need for fancy, for flights of imagination, springs from the inadequacy of perception where human relations are concerned. Mere physical evidence about another being does not tell us what we need to know: we must inform it with our own inner world. And singing out loud—as silly as it sounds—enables us to internalize this lesson more deeply.

Live Your Own Masterpiece

Some years ago our friend David was given an unexpected Christmas present. He and his family were spending the holiday in New York with their friends Henry and Deborah, who have a great capacity for friendship. This Christmas promised to be one of the best ever. As the two families emerged from midnight mass at St. Luke's Church in Greenwich Village, Henry turned to David with a twinkle in his eye and said, "You certainly belted out those carols. I think I've just found the perfect Christmas present for you!" Henry, a professional opera singer, gave David six singing lessons with a coach from the Metropolitan Opera.

David's face, recalls his wife, Caroline, was a hilarious mixture of delight and horror when the gift was revealed. "I can't waste her time. I mean . . . I have no talent!" But eventually, with some trepidation, David went for his first lesson. The voice coach—a wonderful teacher who commuted between Paris and New York—was delighted to put him through his paces. First, scales to loosen him up. Eventually she taught him to sing a few eighteenth-century Italian arias.

These lessons changed David's life. No, he didn't start singing at the world's major opera houses, but the way he looked at himself did change. His life became pregnant with possibility—all because an imaginative and generous friend had dared to give him what he didn't dare claim for himself. There was no way David, on his own, would have sought out singing lessons. But after enjoying his amazing Christmas present, he looked at his life differently, seeing it as a work in progress—a work of art! That gift was a springtime event.

Living your life as a work of art may sound inflated, but it's a way of giving voice to your unique story. Many of us get to know the drama and cast of characters inside us through therapy. We pay someone to listen to our story, and he or she helps us identify the voices on the tape we play to ourselves as we go about our lives. Therapy can be important in digging out the raw material of the drama, but turning it into art requires economy, selection, and discipline of form. Practicing gratitude helps to shape our story in the most creative ways. When we treat our experience as a gift, worlds of possibility open up before us. We find that we have a distinct song to sing and a part to play, and our singing and acting become the route to a deeper reality.

Don't let anything stand in the way of your work in progress. The possibility of spring is always available to you.

Sing Thanks

We can all sing. It is our birthright. Our personal song is peculiar to us and yet blends with all the other voices of creation. St. Francis of Assisi sang of creation and saw every creature and natural event— sun and moon, earth, fire and water, even death—as a brother or sister. His *Canticle of the Sun* rejoices in simply being alive with all other created things. The simple spiritual maxim goes, "Being is communion"—to be fully alive is to be connected, we might even say wellconnected.

Why is it important—to others as well as to ourselves—that we find and share our creation song? Because each of us, like every organism on the planet, contributes to life on earth. Sometimes it's hard to see ourselves as significant in this very much larger picture. It can be overwhelming, in fact, and lead people to despair of their life's purpose. It's a problem as old as human consciousness, and for many people, turning to religious faith (God knows why I'm here, even if I don't) is the only comfort. In today's world we are rightfully fearful of our species' potential to ravage the planet, so the temptation to see ourselves as a burden rather than a gift to creation can be stronger than ever, and traditional forms of faith can be harder to come by.

But some leap of faith is essential—a belief that we have reason to be, even if we don't understand it. We might consider the arguments of conservationists, who fight to keep species from being exterminated even when no "useful" purpose for their existence can be discerned.

Simply put, there is so much we don't (and maybe cannot) know, despite our scientific prowess. And mere utility can be a spiritual dead end. Like the lilies in the Bible that do not toil or spin but are only beautiful, we have a place in life more basic and mysterious than our deeds. Creation is pure gift. And our response to that pure gift can only be gratitude.

When we find our own music, sing our own song, give of ourselves completely to others or to our work and our passions, we are acknowledging the great gift of existence and saying thank you. It doesn't really matter whether we choose to address our thanks to a creator. If there is a God, the divine will approve of this way of living. Perhaps more to the point, the rest of creation, especially your human fellow travelers, will respond gratefully, creatively, lovingly. And your personal story, fully lived, joins and enriches the greater human drama; your private music becomes part of the vast symphony of creation.

So then, what are the essentials in expanding our gratitude practice to singing thanks for creation? Our real music making as human beings is enjoyed, achieved, and celebrated only through:

- Opening up to the possibility of the genuinely new, the ecstatic experience, the rebirth of spring
- The salutary pain of catharsis, of being broken open, welcoming the tears and pain of change
- The power of art to help us renegotiate reality and give us a generous construction of the seen
- The emotional shock of surrendering to love (both intimacy and simple caring for others)
- Allowing our deepest selves to be known, our unique song to be heard, by those around us

We also need to laugh at ourselves and our efforts to craft, sculpt, or compose our lives according to our vision of what they should be. That vision inevitably changes, often rendering earlier efforts laughable. And the unexpected gift, coming in many guises, may radically revise our approach. The poet W. H. Auden described life as a very grand opera played by a tenth-rate touring company!

Gratitude Practice: Composing Your Song of Creation

1. Start writing your own creation story, from the beginning of time to the latest moment of your own existence. Use broad strokes. Borrow whatever appeals to you from creation physics, evolution science, Christian theology, Native American or other creation myths. Use whatever you know about your own heritage to imagine how your distant ancestors came together, and sketch in the rough outlines of your family and personal history. Don't get bogged down in research and detail. You're aiming to write not more than 500 words or so—just a couple of pages. If you do this in even the quickest, sketchiest way, you still will have a document that tells an astounding tale. Looking at it, you will be struck by how absolutely remarkable it is that you exist at all, and you will have given your existence a shape that no one else can.

2. If meditation is congenial to you, try meditating on this idea: *The universe is glad you are here.*

3. Tell someone else that you feel grateful for his or her existence.

4. Try your hand—or your voice—at something you've never attempted. Read a poem or part of a short story aloud. Read to a child. Make something with clay or yarn or watercolor or markers. Learn a dance step. Memorize a tune from a recording and sing it in the shower. Sing an old nursery rhyme. "Conduct" a symphony concert you hear on the radio. Recite the Gettysburg Address or another famous speech. This doesn't have to be the start of an ambitious new pastime; it's only a way to marvel briefly at what you the human animal is capable of. Try not to be too judgmental about your results. And whenever you take on a new challenge in the future, try to see it as another chance to sing creation.

5. Tell something true about yourself: to a coworker, a friend, your mate, your child. It doesn't have to be a deep, dark secret, and it shouldn't be something that will be a burden to them. But tell them something real: a fact from your history that shaped you or how you felt about an experience the two of you shared. This gift is something of yourself.

Because we are ever-evolving creatures, the worst word about us is never the last word. So when you get up in the morning and look in the mirror, do you love, admire, and celebrate what you see? It takes practice, but little by little you will find your voice because you have something to sing about.

3

Meeting Nature in the Flesh

Something hidden. Go and find it.
Go and look beyond the Ranges—
Something lost behind the Ranges.
Lost and waiting for you. Go!
      —RUDYARD KIPLING

John's friend Anna used to tell him about her adventures in nature—
that is, the natural events she witnessed in the San Francisco city
park where she walked her dog twice a day. More than once she stood
and watched enthralled as hawks cruised the tiny park for prey, until
they were spotted and mobbed by the local blackbird gang and forced
to decamp. Every year in April, a sunny, southeast-facing slope—what
it faced was a grim housing project and San Francisco Bay—would
sprout neon orange clumps of poppies amidst the grass made lush by
winter rains. The same slope, five months earlier, would have been
barren and blackened by fire-safety burns. One December, a record-
breaking windstorm howled its way through the night, through the
eucalyptus and pines, and deep into her memory; her walk the next
morning was through a landscape littered with bark, limbs, and other
reminders of nature's power.

It was a small thing, though, that moved Anna the most. Among
many birds the park hosted, the shyest were the flickers—large, brown
insect eaters of the underbrush. When disturbed, a flicker would
instantly take flight for the taller branches, in the process flashing the
warm rust-colored underside of its wings. "I don't know why," says

Anna, "but every time I saw that flash of color, even just out of the corner of my eye, something went through me like a scalpel straight to the heart. It never failed. I still don't understand it."

This specific event surely affected Anna in her own way, but all veteran birdwatchers have experienced something similar. The purest visual equivalent to the ecstatic moment of going live may be a bird taking flight—a sudden, miraculous lifting out of the ordinary and earthbound into joyful liberation and limitless imagination.

In fact, the stab of aliveness we've talked about—that instant when we are overtaken by wonder—seems to come most reliably at times where we're in direct contact with nature, with as much filtering as possible stripped away. "Think of our life in nature," Thoreau urged in *The Maine Woods,* "daily to be shown matter, to come in contact with it—rocks, trees, wind on our cheeks! the *solid* earth! the *actual* world! the *common sense! Contact! Contact!*"

Any of us can summon up such moments, even if we've done most of our hiking in urban canyons. Glancing out a high-rise window to see the season's first snowfall, or inhaling the sharp, ionized air after a violent spring thunderstorm. Passing trees glazed in crystal after an ice storm. Spotting a brilliantly blooming cactus on a stark desert trail. Cresting a mountain pass, when suddenly your hemmed-in view opens out for miles in all directions. The way time enters another dimension while we sit beside a flowing stream.

Nature's breathtaking phenomena and artful patterns have always encouraged the sense that some spiritual force, if not divine intent, is at work in the world. Sand dollars, bird plumage, spiderwebs, butterfly wings, milkweed globes, lichen painting, wood graining, fern lacing, ocean-carved rock, flower petaling—all so much more subtle and intricate than human ingenuity could conceive. Bioluminescent organisms on tropical waters; fireflies blinking on a woodland edge. The sound of the wind and the feel of soft rain on one's face. Smells: pine forest in summer heat, or the complex and pungent perfume of low tide. (A friend recalls, "I went to look at a house I was thinking of renting, and as I got out of the car I was enveloped by the scent of sage. I knew right then I would take the house, no matter what.")

Thoreau heads a long list of writers who eloquently describe the grateful unfolding of the human spirit in nature. It's a well-worked theme, from Gilbert Selborne botanizing in his seventeenth-century English meadows to Annie Dillard at Tinker Creek, from John Muir clambering up the flanks of Yosemite waterfalls to Peter Matthiessen pursuing snow leopards and salvation in the Himalaya, or reporter Jon Krakauer struggling with the eternal, fatal lure of Everest. Throughout the diverse literature of the outdoors, some consistent qualities emerge about nature's gifts and our responses to them.

Big Experience or Big Letdown?

This spot where you sit is your own spot. It is on this very spot and in this very moment that you can become enlightened. You don't have to sit beneath a special tree in a distant land.
— THICH NHAT HANH

It's clear, for one thing, that enlivening contact with nature is an experience that's available almost anywhere, not just in spectacular, remote, or expensive-to-get-to places. It's just as possible in a city park or an old farm field or around a summer cabin as it is on a trek in Nepal, rafting the Amazon, or surfing big waves in Oahu. Of course, anyone fortunate enough to visit these more exotic natural destinations may indeed find soul-expanding epiphanies there. But despite the travel industry's seductive marketing, transcendence is not exclusively available to those who can pay a premium for it. By far, the more important coin is the quality of attention we pay to what's around us.

Rachel Carson, who ushered in modern-day environmentalism with her crusading book *Silent Spring,* derived her passion for the natural world from her own experience and study of the stretch of Maine coastline she called home. She could write magnificently and movingly even about plankton, because she spent time observing the workings of nature close at hand. In her small book *The Sense of Wonder,* she describes introducing her small nephew to the woods and waters of her homeland. "If I had influence with the good fairy who is supposed to preside over the christening of all children," she writes, "I should ask that her gift to each child in the world be a sense of wonder so indestructible that it would last throughout life, as an unfailing antidote against the boredom and disenchantments of later years, the sterile preoccupation with things that are artificial, the alienation from the sources of our strength."

Trusting that ordinary glimpses of nature can yield extraordinary rewards goes against the cultural grain today, when measures of worth are ruthlessly calculated in terms of expense, rarity, and exclusivity. People will fly across the world to witness a total eclipse or a dramatic meteor shower, yet never think to lie outdoors on the grass taking in the night sky on an everyday summer evening. And if the Big Event leaves us with a sense of anticlimax, that can be hard to admit even to ourselves—after all, we were privileged to be there, so it had to be special, right?

Well, not really. Because when we go in straight-line pursuit of transcendence—when we try to manage it, control it, schedule it, package it—that's when it is most likely to elude us. Or to turn it around: that which makes us feel most alive is that over which we have the least control. Nowhere do we see this more clearly than in experiencing nature. You can sign up for an East African safari, and the outfitter can guarantee that X number of animals will show up at a waterhole. Or vacation at a Hawaiian megahotel that offers the chance to swim with dolphins in a manmade lagoon.

But an ecstatic moment in nature is more likely to sneak up on you unprepared. Usually the best you can hope to do is put yourself in the way of a possible experience—which is what people do in going to wild places. But the more controlled the setting, the more like a theme park it is, the less probable that your encounter with nature will plumb the depths of your heart. That's why zoos, however useful for study, are no substitute for seeing wild animals on their own ground, unfenced and uncontrolled.

Naturalist and writer Paul Gruchow describes a hiking trip in the Montana mountains in which a female grizzly bear and her cubs invaded his campsite without warning. He and his companion could only watch in awe as the great bear took possession of their little outpost of civilization and destroyed most of it looking for food:

> The bear used the same foothold I had used to get up one of the anchor trees, stretched her massive right front paw, its long claws glinting, ten feet up, seized the rope, and thwacked it up and down

until John's pack slid toward her. . . . She ripped apart the packs and searched the scattered contents, item by item, for edibles . . . she overlooked nothing. . . . We watched her at close range for some time, spellbound and joyful. In our helplessness we had lost our fear. It felt liberating to be, for once, in charge of absolutely nothing.

So despite enduring a major fright, loss of property, and the inconvenience of having to cut their trip short, Gruchow and his friend felt grateful for the encounter. Grateful, of course, to have come through it safely. But more grateful for the contact with a magnificent creature, a big mammal that has symbolized power and cleverness for many human cultures. And through her, contact with our fellow humans from past ages who lived on a more equal footing with other beings on the earth.

Making It Real

Now I see the secret of making of the best of persons. It is to grow in the open air, and to eat and sleep with the earth.
     —WALT WHITMAN, *LEAVES OF GRASS*

I would say the real play is in the act of going totally off the trail— away from any trace of human or animal regularity aimed at some practical or spiritual purpose.
     —GARY SNYDER

Robert Michael Pyle wrote in *The Thunder Tree* about the "extinction of experience" being as troubling as the extinction of species. He is talking about personal alienation from nature, our lack of a sense of intimacy with the natural world, even as people watch nature documentaries and talk about wanting to save the planet. "When the natural world becomes chiefly an entertainment or an obligation," he writes, "it loses its ability to arouse our deeper instincts." Only the direct experience of nature can arouse our gratitude.

Our friends Sarah, Margaret, and Al took a quick midweek trip to Yosemite in early October 2001. They're all over sixty: Sarah's retired (except for teaching accordion lessons); Margaret and Al are busy musicians with demanding day jobs. Like most of us, they were still feeling raw and unsettled by the events of September 2001 and seized the chance to get out of their city life for a few days. Sarah says,

> It was so great. Margaret and I took the easy hike up Vernal Falls Trail. It's short but I'd forgotten how steep—we were really proud of ourselves for making it all the way, even with our bum knees. Al's in better shape, and he took a longer route. But, oh my God, we met some wonderful people and we soaked up the air, the smells, the river sounds. Later we drove up to Tuolumne Meadows and just wandered around. Heavenly!

And a different story: Dave, a corporate attorney and weekend wind-surfing warrior, just got back from Hood River, Oregon, mecca of the boardsailing world. Taking advantage of the up-to-50-mph winds that howl down the Columbia Gorge, expert windsurfers slice across the half-mile-wide span of the Columbia River. It was Dave's first time there:

> I made it all the way across so I was pretty happy. What you don't want to do is capsize midway, because if the big boats in the shipping channel can't see your sail, you could be done for. I love the sport because you're working with the wind and you're in direct contact with the water—you do have some control but you have to go with the conditions, which are pretty fierce there.

So here are perhaps two extremes of nature recreation. There's a lot of polarization today in the great arena of "enjoying the outdoors." Those who favor less strenuous ways of being in nature tend to get riled at the mountain bikers zipping down their trails and the skiers who live for speed. The seriously fit thrill seekers, for their part, sometimes feel discriminated against.

From our point of view, it doesn't matter which path into nature you choose, as long as you go. Go for what's possible based on where you are, your level of fitness, and your tolerance of physical stress. Going slowly and quietly can yield certain gifts you might otherwise miss: a closer glimpse of wildlife, a leisurely, soul-opening conversation. But for those who are capable, testing oneself physically in the outdoors can provide a rush that no movie or thrill ride can approach.

Spiking the tonic of the outdoors with physical risk taking—as in mountaineering or hiking in areas frequented by big carnivores—can sharpen that knife edge of aliveness.

How you choose to experience nature (within regulations) is a personal choice. It may even be a compulsion the seeker doesn't entirely understand. George Leigh Mallory, who died trying to climb Mount Everest in 1921, famously answered "because it is there" to the question "Why climb the mountain?" But he also said something much less enigmatic. "What we get from this adventure," he explained, "is just sheer joy. And joy is, after all, the end of life."

The Grateful Response

How do we express gratitude for the enlivenings we get from nature? Some people give thanks for nature's gifts through direct action, contributing their time and effort on behalf of preservation; many more write checks to conservation groups, buy organic produce, or recycle their newspapers and bottles. A friend of ours likes to voice his gratitude aloud in church: "Let us give thanks for old trees and high mountains and clean rivers, and pray for the wisdom to safeguard them." Others make a point of "voting green"—for candidates who support environmental protection or initiatives that fund open spaces. A few of those who care passionately put themselves at risk for what they believe: standing in the path of chainsaws like Julia Butterfly Hill, the young woman who spent two years in the branches of a redwood.

There might be still more personal ways to acknowledge the complex relationship we twenty-first-century humans have with the earth's natural systems. We know that transcendent experiences of aliveness can be found in wild nature, and we are grateful for those reminders that we are connected to the greater web of life on the planet. But humans don't inhabit the Garden anymore. We are resource exploiters, and there's no going back. Most of us eat stock animals and cultivated grains, consume petroleum and other fossil fuels, and enjoy all the conveniences made possible by human brainpower applied to natural resources. Even if we are conscientious recyclers or vegetarians or don't wear leather, there's no getting away from this entirely.

Beyond doing what we can, both in private life and public policy, to preserve natural resources, how could we cultivate a better give and take with the gifts earth provides for our survival and pleasure? For one thing, we can face our consumption honestly, looking beyond the processing and packaging to see clearly the food-raising or timber-harvesting practices that bring us such bounty. Our habit of dissociating what we eat or use from its original sources is guilt producing—and gratitude doesn't cohabit well with guilt.

We must recognize the impact on a healthy environment of the choices we make in our lives. Change them for the better if we can. And, if possible, reinvest our consumption with elements of the sacred—like Native Americans and others who have important rituals connected with harvesting crops and slaying animals for food.

We can devise our own rituals of thanks that acknowledge that our food and other resources come from somewhere other than a warehouse. Thanksgiving rituals around food can be joyful as well as solemn, as we'll see in a later chapter. We'll mention one here: writer and fly-fisherman David Duncan's recipe for "spirit-fried" trout. One of just two ingredients for this dish, he notes, is real butter.

> Wild trout frying is not a meal, it's a rite. You are preparing to eat an animal that gave up its beautiful river and only life for your pleasure. Pleasure ought, therefore, to be maximized. Open your palate to the trout's flavor and your heart to its riverine essence, and that essence will charge through you like spring runoff, flushing every artery you've got. It is never "heart smart" to refuse to open your heart.

Even food bought at the supermarket is worthy of a ritual of thanks. And if you can grow or catch some of your own (unendangered) food, or buy it from local growers at a farmer's market, and enjoy it in your reasonably energy-efficient home . . . then so much the better for your sense of giving something back to the natural world.

Passing the Torch

If your experiences in nature have brought joy, made you feel alive, and provoked gratitude, the best way to respond thankfully is to bring someone else into the experience—preferably a child. Sociobiologist

Edmund O. Wilson popularized a theory that humans have an innate desire to connect with other life forms, which he calls "biophilia," and that exercising this instinct is therapeutic. But to engage our biophilia we need direct exposure. Most American kids today have too little opportunity for contact with nature, and too much chance to settle for what they see on TV. "What is the extinction of a condor," asks Michael Pyle, "to a child who has never known a wren?"

Rachel Carson, in teaching her young nephew to know and love the Maine coast, knew that she was passing on a great gift:

> What is the value of preserving and strengthening this sense of awe and wonder, this recognition of something beyond the boundaries of human existence? . . . Those who dwell, as scientists or laymen, among the beauties and mysteries of the earth are never alone or weary of life. Whatever the vexations and concerns of their personal lives, their thoughts can find paths that lead to inner contentment and renewed excitement in living. Those who contemplate the beauty of the earth find reserves of strength that will endure as long as life lasts. . . . There is something infinitely healing in the repeated refrains of nature—the assurance that dawn comes after night, and spring after the winter.

Our suggestion for a gratitude practice? Go gratefully to meet nature in the flesh, as often as you can, and the world will be richer.

4

Celebrating Our Genes

I am the family face
Flesh perishes; I live on.
—THOMAS HARDY

Blood Ties

Acknowledging the gifts we receive by way of family is a vital part of psychological maturation and spiritual development. In past societies, celebrating blood ties was as natural and inevitable as breathing, absorbed from infancy through family and tribal rituals, faithfully practiced, passed down in oft-told stories and sacred objects (think of the tiny ancestor carvings that the hero in the movie *Gladiator* cherished and guarded throughout his enslavement).

In times past, the gift of life was forever threatened by illness, war, famine, and natural perils; the mysteries of genetic inheritance could be witnessed but not analyzed; and our sense of friend and foe was local rather than global. In such times, it was natural for people to bless their ancestors for the survival of their line, demonstrate gratitude to family allies on whom their security might rest, and reinforce their special distinctions from other tribes through art and ritual.

How we experience and express gratitude for our family heritage is more complex and thorny. Whom do we thank for the fundamental gift of life in an age of designer drugs, replaceable parts, and in vitro conceptions? How do we sustain gratitude for a genetic heritage that may contain genes for alcoholism, heart disease, or bipolar disorder? What happens to gratitude in a culture of victimization, where one can blame the family legacy for neurotic complexes (at best) or outright abuse (at worst)? And how do we nurture strong family ties when generations are distanced by continents and oceans, when the extended family is the exception?

Every family has its own rich story, which is fed by the culture in which the family grows. If we try to deny the truth of this story, we put our true selves in peril and cut ourselves off from the possibility of gratitude for our heritage.

Among the questions we'll consider in this chapter are: Where does gratitude fit in the complex web of responses we have to our families, both immediate and distant? Why is it important to honor family heritage, and what lessons can we take from the examples of other cultures? How do we discover what our "family values" are and treasure them? How does honoring cultural/spiritual traditions—attending a Seder, going on pilgrimage to Mecca, worshiping at high mass on Easter, or joining in a Buddhist retreat—help shape who we are and aspire to be?

The Genetic Gift and the Hand of History

The fact of genetic inheritance has been known much longer than it has been understood. Families once counted on identifying certain physical traits in their offspring—red hair, a distinctive nose, the famous Hapsburg lip—to assure themselves of the fidelity of spouses and make certain that property would be passed down to the officially designated heir. At some point, too, it became apparent that curses as well as blessings could be a family inheritance: the blood disease hemophilia, for instance.

In the few decades since we have begun to unravel the genetic code, we've gotten a better picture of just how wondrous it is—one of the primary ordering systems of existence, the organizing principle for all life on earth. Genetic inheritance is pure gift, one of the "givens" we must accept because we can do very little about it.

If genetic code is the native clay of our lives, experience is the potter's hands that form it on the wheel, and the kiln that fires it. The hands that shape us first and most lastingly are those of our parents, and sometimes other family members: the nurture half of the nature/nurture divide. Our unique personal histories, acting upon our genetic clay, are what cause us as adults to see ourselves as privileged or victim, cherished or abandoned, capable or helpless. Beyond our genes we are given stories and messages about how lovable we are or how optimistic we should be.

Analyzing the ways in which our families shaped us for good or ill is an important part of coming to self knowledge. The facts of the matter—Dad left us, Mom was an alcoholic, Grandma thought I was the greatest thing that ever came along, my brother was always the high achiever, or any of a million such vital facts—must be acknowledged at some point in our personal development. But it is our response to these facts that determines what our lives will be.

If we were nurtured in positive ways, gratitude is always an appropriate response. If our parents or other caretakers failed us in large and obvious ways, gratitude may take more practice! But we also know plenty of folks who cannot see where gratitude is due, even when their familial blessings are manifold and evident to the world.

When wealth and privilege enter the picture, the flow of gratitude between generations often becomes confused and muddied. Rather than learning to value the gifts of good parenting and rich community, many children of the privileged get the sense that they should show gratitude mainly for material blessings and social advantages: gifts that are worth something but whose worth is blown out of proportion.

The sense of entitlement that too often comes with privilege is lethal to gratitude—its shadow side. If we accept as a birthright gifts that set us apart—beauty, wealth, social standing, power—without seeking ways to express gratitude for them, we become dangerous not only to others but to ourselves. Recognizing this, ancient cultures evolved countering rituals to reduce the effects of bestowed privilege, focusing credit on ancestors rather than the living, who might harm their society and lose their souls.

Rituals and the Power of Cultural DNA

Rituals that honor those who came before us, whose genetic code we possess, help us toward a healthy practice of gratitude. Even if our family legacy is a mixed blessing, family-honoring rituals carried out in good faith can help us transcend confusion and ambivalence about our past, make sense of our personal histories, help us find our bearings, and anchor us in the greater human family to which we all belong.

In the rest of this chapter we'll look at examples of such rituals—some from non-Western or past cultures, some from families in twenty-first-century America who have made deliberate efforts to sustain family ties through rituals that blend gracefully into contemporary life. These examples show how values and beliefs are passed along, and how learning can accrue.

Family rituals, whether holiday celebrations, food traditions, artistic expressions, or patterns of worship, always emerge from a cultural context, even if that context is fragmented by the pace of modern life. Trying to divorce oneself completely from that cultural context can severely stress one's capacity for gratitude.

Sometimes the traditions of other cultures seem exotically attractive and more authentic than our own, perhaps even possessing magical powers. But while we may gain insight from experimenting with them, or adapt certain ideas, we suggest that trying to adopt them whole hog may prove only temporarily satisfying and not sustainable.

Each culture has encoded lessons to pass on that give successive generations a sense of what came before and why such knowledge is useful. Here are a few of the lessons in gratitude that are available through traditional practices.

SINGING AND DANCING

Singing, chanting, and movement are powerful tools for sustaining community. By joining in such rituals community members internalize their ancestral myths, shared dreams, creation stories, and world-ordering beliefs. In sacred dancing—from the Sufi tradition to Indian and Southeast Asian forms to the Sioux Sun Dance—each generation relies on past masters to teach them the steps and hand down the mysteries.

Such rituals also can open communication between peoples and generations. Gene and Freda Kalache, social entrepreneurs from Colorado Springs, sponsored a 1998 symposium on the arts of tribal healing, which brought together Native American shamans with Chinese healers. Although participants were separated by language, they seemed to have little trouble communicating via chant and body movement to share longstanding traditions of healing the body and spirit. The sensory aspect of these rituals—employing sound vibrations, vigorous movement and gentle touching, the scent of burning herbs—helped transcend cultural barriers.

Modern rituals based on music and dance can likewise stimulate contact across distances of age and honor our elders. Families that share music on a regular basis tend to have strong intergenerational bonds. One friend of ours has been folk dancing with his parents—and his grandparents, while they were alive—since he and his brother were children; they also gather on weekends to play in informal early-music quartets. When a groom or groomsman dances with the grandmother at a wedding, bringing her physically into the center of the family, both she and the young man are honored.

TOTEMS AND CLANS

Among native tribes around the Pacific Rim, carving totems and masks was a way to celebrate links between current and past generations. Totem poles, and the masks used in totem rituals, contain the images of animals that explain creation, honor ancestors, or represent virtues. A totem pole reflects tribal unity, cultural values, and personal wisdom to be acquired and honored. This tradition of artisanship is enjoying a vigorous revival.

Each carved figure represents an ancestor spirit and its part in the story of human survival and spiritual intervention. Members of a clan believe they are descended from a totem ancestor and thus are all brothers in, say, the raven or the eagle clan. Birds were common figures, and according to Jung they represent the phoenix, symbol of rebirth and rejuvenation; his own family coat of arms contained one. Jung wrote, "I feel strongly that I am under the influence of things or questions which were left incomplete and unanswered by my parents and grandparents and more distant ancestors. It often seems as if there were an impersonal karma within a family . . . passed on from parents to children."

A major arts event in 1994 at Stanford University featured a group of handsome young men from Papua New Guinea carving massive totem poles. The carvers' skill with their razor-sharp axes, the lovely images telling a creation story, the shared act—all became mesmerizing theater. No watcher could miss the powerful meta-message: honoring ancestral exploits and sharing stories is profoundly important in developing community values and celebrating life.

FAMILY SAINTS AND SPIRIT GUIDES

The ancient Romans practiced ancestor worship, centered on the concept of a genius (*gens*) of the family—an inner spirit passed on from one generation to another. This *genius* bound Romans to their ancestors and their descendants in a single sustained community. Masks and carved figures of the family hearth gods were part of this cult.

Revering powerful ancestor spirits has been important in many other societies, from West Africa to China to Scandinavia. Ancestors are believed to wield great authority, having special powers to influence events or the well-being of their living relatives. Protection of the family is a primary concern. Ancestors are considered intermediaries between the supreme god, or gods, and the people, and can communicate with the living through dreams and by possession.

The idea of a unifying, protecting family spirit has mostly been lost in later European traditions. Likewise the communal effort of creating artful objects that stand for family values. For centuries the wealthy turned over the task of memorializing their forebears to portrait painters, and lived with the results glowering down at them from the walls of the family manse.

Today we honor family members by displaying photographs around the house and in albums, or sometimes we make videos. A friend's brother-in-law is handy with the videocamera, and has made a point of sitting down with his father to coax memories and stories from him so the grandchildren will have access to some family history through this medium.

Some people believe that their ability to practice an ancient or esoteric craft comes from an ancestor spirit. A woman we know says she adopted her great-grandmother as a spirit guide. "My grandmother's mother, Ruthann, homesteaded in North Dakota with her husband, raised eight children, farmed, propagated and sold sunflower seeds, made just about all of her family's clothing. I think I'm the only one in my family who's done any serious sewing since then, and I've always felt a bond with her. I only know her from pictures and a few inscriptions. But when I feel sort of beaten down, I try to think of her and what she had to deal with. It helps to know I've got some of her blood and her strength in me."

Many people set aside a special place in the home for objects that honor family members—they may or may not call that place a shrine. A Boston public relations consultant created a spot in the hallway of her home to assemble her most precious keepsakes. On a Queen Anne sideboard, she placed a ceramic bowl given to her by a close friend; candlesticks brought from Ghana by her daughter; photos of her grandfather, father, and uncle, of herself and her brother; and an old leather suitcase that once belonged to her grandfather. "In my home, it's where the people that I'm connected to, my progenitors, live. They still live for me so I keep a space for them," she says.

FAMILY HOLIDAYS

Traditional religious holidays, or "holy days," are occasions for families and communities to commemorate cultural history and renew sacred bonds, through rituals that often involve special foods or objects, the lighting of candles or fires, and sometimes visits or pilgrimages. The Jewish festivals of Chanukah and Passover are good examples, most often occasions for warm family gatherings, both solemn and festive. In Catholic families, individuals often have a patron saint whose day is celebrated; a way of connecting to one's spiritual roots on a regular basis.

The late fall observances of All Souls' Day and All Saints' Day (Allhallows') are Christian days of revering the saints and praying for all souls in purgatory. They coincide with an ancient pagan festival of the dead called Samhain, whose darkly powerful rituals marked the end of harvest and the coming of winter (death). Somehow all these have evolved into the costume and candy orgy of Halloween.

In Latin America, October 31 is known as Day of the Dead, an important holiday to honor ancestors that mingles Roman Catholic and Native American traditions. On Dia de los Muertos, Mexicans decorate their homes with playful imagery of animated human skeletons, leave food offerings for wandering spirits, and tend the graves of relatives. Crafting a family altar, or *offrenda,* around Day of the Dead, using photos and memorabilia, is a simple but powerful act that all generations can take part in.

Our Thanksgiving remains a day when we feast in gratitude for family and other blessings. Christmas, despite its insistent commercial messages, is still a time for families to gather from far and wide, ritually braving snowed-in airports and icy highways. Mother's Day, Father's Day, and the less-observed Grandparents' Day all hold possibilities for imaginative, meaningful ways to celebrate our genes, beyond the basic necktie or breakfast on a tray.

Ethnic holidays like Columbus Day can be times for the descendants of immigrants to remember the gifts they've inherited through their families' uprooting and resettling. And holidays that commemorate our war dead can be occasions for trips to a memorial like the Vietnam Wall, or other gestures that honor family members who died in wartime.

RITUALS OF PASSAGE

Baptisms, circumcisions, bar and bat mitzvahs, weddings, major anniversaries, funerals—all these should be conscious occasions for gathering the generations and honoring family bonds. Ideally, they also reinforce the individual's and the family's grounding in a larger community, though these days this is hard to come by outside of church circles.

Coming-of-age rituals are especially important in helping young people make the transition to full participation in community life, but outside of Judaism they are currently in short supply. One progressive church community has instituted—at the urging of its younger members—a sort of quest ritual in which twelve- and thirteen-year-olds choose an adult (not a relation) as a companion on an overnight group camping adventure. The whole community then celebrates a special service—with candles, readings, and parading of the honorees on hoisted chairs—at the completion of the quest.

Visiting the Dead

Making periodic visits to the family graves was once a comforting ritual for most families. It's hard to say exactly when American cemeteries became places to be avoided. Maybe it's because they are often so generic, sterile, and physically isolated from the heart of the community, or because recent generations recoil in horror from the whole idea of aging, death, and decay.

This is a shame. The simple act of traveling to a gravesite, spending one's time quietly communing with loved ones who have passed on, can be soothing and soul enlarging. It is a giving of oneself with no hope of reward and is thus a pure gift. It is also a perfect occasion for gratitude—not just for the life and the DNA of that ancestor, but for the opportunity to break one's busy routine with a meditative visit. Of course, the emotional impact of such a visit can be strong if the loss was close or recent; ideally several family members should make the visit together for mutual comfort.

Some people also find rewards in visiting the resting places of family members they did not know personally, or in making a pilgrimage to the grave of someone they admire greatly. The Père Lachaise cemetery outside of Paris, final home of many famed writers, artists, and musicians, is a frequent site of such pilgrimages.

Flowers, with their symbolically ephemeral beauty, are a traditional part of honoring the dead. For a writer from Hawaii, flowers for the dead were integral to her community life growing up in Hilo. When she visited her grandmother's grave last year, a trio of sisters had recently reopened their family's floral business; they insisted on not only filling her order for the gravesite, but on packing a big box of local blooms for her to take home. "When I was a child," she writes, "[the cemetery] was surrounded by cane fields and much smaller. Now it covers both sides of the road. What strikes me, as always, are the flowers, an entire hillside ablaze with them. The dead are well remembered in Hilo, and the Ebesus have been part of that remembering for many years."

Rituals that Infuse Gratitude into Family Life

Finally, we will explore some contemporary and personal rituals of gratitude within families. The families introduced below have designed gatherings to celebrate their roots and each other. Such rituals can vary from fishing trips and picnics to golf tournaments or major treks to exotic places. Sometimes the effort is highly organized, with carefully arranged activities and entertainment. In other cases it is informal and easygoing. But they all have certain qualities in common, and toward the end we've supplied a checklist.

The Barn Dance

The Rockway family has used an old barn (now refurbished) on their inherited farm for four generations of spring dances. The preparation is divided up: different family members arrange music, food, decoration, photography, entertainment, and cleanup. Bales of hay serve as seating and bases for plywood tables. The current patriarch and matriarch are given special roles, and grandchildren offer skits and songs. Close friends are invited to join in.

Photographs of previous dances are on display, enabling the children to see their great-grandparents dancing in the same barn. There are always speeches: short, corny, and honorific. Each generation is heard from. The theme is celebrating springtime, and the timing is usually arranged around spring break at the kids' schools. But the real event is the love shared among all who join together in this special community of extended family.

The Extended Picnic

Since 1936, two families, the Luvaks and the Sterns, have gathered at a small lake in Canada for an annual spring picnic. The combined "cousins" now number 136, including spouses. As with most modern Canadian families, they are scattered around the world, but each spring many of them find their way to the picnic. The actual reunion lasts three days, with lots of other features: hiking and bike expeditions, boating, and trips to town. But the one-day lakeside gathering is the heart of the affair.

Games, toy boat races, and kite flying are part of the day's ritual. Food and drink are plentiful. As the sun sets, a bonfire is lighted, and all gather close for the core of this ritual. Traditional songs are sung, toasts are made, and silent prayers are offered to those who aren't there in the flesh. The youngest and the oldest are saluted with family songs and cheers.

What's special about these gatherings is the explicit gratitude expressed to those "from whom we came." The pioneers who founded these families immigrated from Russia and joined forces to plant wheat on their neighboring farms. Although few family members still speak Russian, all sing a Russian song to celebrate those hardy farmers who believed in a new land and made life there flourish.

The Habitat for Our Humanity

Five members of the Robinson family signed up on their own one year to work on a Habitat for Humanity building project. After comparing notes, they decided to be a bit more organized and adventuresome the next year. By year four they had recruited a whole crew of cousins and uncles and aunts and were off to a barrio outside San Diego. Three generations participated, using a small inheritance to pay for materials. "The funds came from grandmother Mildred," Bill Robinson explains, "and the project is dedicated to her."

Now, after many years of volunteering, the family albums are filled with pictures of "their" crew and "their" houses. They have continued to dedicate their work to relatives who have passed as a way of remembering them and are adding to Mildred's fund so the next generation can continue the tradition. Bill Robinson adds, "We like to think of what we're doing for others as building our *own* humanity."

What works for this family is work on behalf of others. For the Robinsons, the key to a grateful ritual is "doing something tangible as a family for someone in need. By coming together each spring we also reaffirm our family bonds and celebrate our heritage and our latest members."

A STUDY–WORK CELEBRATION

The annual spring celebration for two families we'll call the Olsons and the Smiths is a blend of study, work, and play. They always gather on the same third weekend in May, usually at the same small resort. "With 162 members it makes the logistics easier," says current family "president" and fourth-generation Swedish immigrant Jed Olson.

Each event has a study theme, and an outside speaker is recruited to lead the discussion. Topics range from family history to the issue of inherited wealth in raising children. Although some of the family members have considerable wealth, others do not. As Jed Olson sees it, "Money could rip this family apart, but by talking openly about the shadows money brings, we at least give ourselves a better chance." He goes on: "Money will always be a problem and a blessing. We are working to be grateful for our inherited wealth rather than resentful if our portion is smaller."

The Olsons work hard at their weekend studies, and they play hard too. The getaway is arranged so that every member can participate. For many it is a reunion with relations they might not see the rest of the year. They take their celebration very seriously. Jed says, "We're all leading busy lives, so this is a once-a-year chance. We agree to remain a family, we celebrate mutual values, and we have lots of fun."

Gratitude Practice: A Short Guide to Family Rituals

Each family should decide how best to use a ritual gathering to honor past members and unite present ones. The choices are wide, but suiting them to each family's profile and resources is essential to success. Here are some basic tips:

1. *Regularity.* Make the ritual into an annual event that people look forward to and put first on their calendars.
2. *Organization.* Pick a small organizing committee carefully and rotate the assignments every three years. Set up a family website to keep in touch (see myfamily.com).
3. *Balance.* Blend the serious and the fun, social purpose and personal satisfaction. Don't let the sober-sided oldsters or the

Bacchus god take over the event. Make sure the youngest generation is represented.

4. *Adaptability.* Learn from others and keep adjusting the program
   based on "customer satisfaction." All good rituals evolve.

5. *Financial responsibility.* Budget generously but be frugal. Make
   sure no family member becomes Mr. or Mrs. Deep Pockets.
   Each member should be allowed to contribute in some way.

6. *Honoring elders.* Make a point of honoring those who come
   before. The more we celebrate across the span of generations,
   the more powerful the ritual.

Finally, try to keep it simple, fun, and loving.

5

Cleaning House

Our house was not unsentient matter—it had a heart and a soul
and eyes to see with; and approvals and solicitudes and deep
sympathies; it was of us, and we were in its confidence and
lived in its grace. . . .
— MARK TWAIN, ON HIS HOME IN HARTFORD, CONNECTICUT

Shelter is one of the essentials of human life, a blessing we find hard
to take for granted even if our lives are relatively comfortable. Just
try to imagine the intense gratitude our prehistoric ancestors felt on
discovering a well-situated cave in which to take refuge from the elements, from dangerous beasts or fellow humans. Think how intensely
we react to the homeless in our midst today, a reaction compounded of
compassion and fear—along with thankfulness that we don't share
their fate.

Expressions of gratitude for the roof over our heads have taken
many forms. In some cultures dwellings are adorned with spiritual symbols: mezuzahs in Jewish doorways, ghost catchers in Bali, food for the
spirits in Africa, herbs and fragrant flowers in Hawaii. Religious traditions offer house blessings and similar ceremonies; occasionally houses
are given rites of exorcism to comfort occupants who feel bedeviled.
Where we choose to live also has been enveloped in ceremony and ritual: animal sacrifice or geomancy have been used to locate or endorse
building sites (which harks back to that well-situated cave).

Today as much as ever, a person's home is his castle, a fortress and
oasis of peace in a frenetic world. If we're lucky, our home is also the

center of our emotional life, the place where we share our most intimate moments with partners and family, and thus inextricably linked
in our hearts with our closest relationships. Even when someone dies,
their presence in a house can live on, as loving widows and widowers
can attest. Sometimes it's a comfort; sometimes the lingering associations are too painful and the survivor must move on.

You and Your Home

There is a private bond between dweller and dwelling—sweat in, satisfaction out. Saturday morning: time to tackle the entry hall floor, the
abused closet, the disastrous refrigerator. As grime and disorganization
give way, our sweat feels decently earned—what John likes to call
"grateful sweat." A freshly polished table topped with a bouquet of daffodils can make as sweet an impression as a Matisse still life.

Recent trends reflect, we think, a growing awareness of this personal bond with our homes, and our desire to make them the center of
an integrated, harmonious life. While there will always be important
work for professional home builders and designers, most recognize that
these days clients want to see their own tastes reflected; many people
elect to take a hands-on role in the design, remodeling, or decorating of
their homes. The pros may not always welcome this, but the smart ones
learn to live with it. The homeowner whose own sweat is in the walls
has that much more of a grateful appreciation for the rewards of home.

Also on the rise is the awareness that the home is part of a larger
environment, and that physical surroundings affect our well-being. All
this is encompassed by the ancient Chinese principles of *feng shui* (literally "wind and water"), which hold that the beneficial and harmful
forces of the universe are manifested in the landscape in ways that are
either harmonious or not. Propitious elements include curving structures and waterways, and places where hills meet lower ground; long,
straight lines and X-shapes are among negative elements. The Chinese
have used feng shui in choosing dwelling sites since the Han dynasty
(200 B.C.). Its principles, elucidated by expert feng shui "doctors," also
guided the development of landscape gardening, one of that culture's
supreme arts.

Simply put, feng shui is based on our innate sensitivity to place and surroundings, our instincts for what feels safe or threatening, soothing or stimulating. Modern practitioners use its principles to suggest the layout of rooms in a home being designed, or the arrangement of furniture and other elements to maximize "good" feng shui in existing structures.

Inside and Outside

It is important to inhabit our most familiar and well-used spaces more consciously—to act on going live to our surroundings. This may mean heightening our appreciation for what's there, or recognizing the need to make changes to improve our quality of life. Gratitude will flow from both.

If this sounds like a way of thinking about our inner spaces, too, we mean it to be. Just as the home contains our physical life, the soul is a dwelling with many rooms, each filled with our personal history: our loves, passions, fears, past careers and relationships, as well as hopes and dreams.

In St. Teresa of Avila's writings about the "Interior Castle," she points out that many of us haven't ventured far inside, for fear of what we might find there. In fact, she claims, most of us have only ventured into the outer courtyard. The rest of this chapter is concerned with exploring connections between our outer and inner homes, and the need to regularly venture deep within the house of the spirit to confront, clean, or renovate what's there.

Spring Cleaning

Even the smallest dwelling can hold a surprising amount, as we discover to our dismay when moving time comes! The challenge, as a feng shui master might put it, is to keep energy moving in your house in healthy ways, to be aware of when things are piling up and blocking energy flow. Know when it's time to take stock, clear away clutter, and deep clean.

Spring is an auspicious time to mark our gratitude for gifts of home with a bout of spring cleaning. In winter, especially in colder climes, we draw inward and hoard our resources, consciously or not. When the first real signs of spring appear, we are deeply stirred to throw open the windows, retire the heavy clothes, and subject our living quarters to massive doses of Windex and Murphy's Oil Soap. Sales of paint and wallpaper are as reliable a sign of spring as swallows heading for San Juan Capistrano. Carting bags off to charity, scrubbing soot off the fireplace, stripping winter's mulch off the garden—these are wonderful moments in which to let gratitude settle on us.

Our souls also need periodic evaluation and spring cleaning. Metaphorically speaking, we need to throw back the curtains, take down our shutters, open up our vistas. We need spiritual replenishing, the glow of fresh beginnings. How do we choose which elements to save or throw away, renovate or replace? What's keeping out the light and the air?

The elements of spring cleaning for the soul are:

- Take stock and open up space
- Find treasures long lost
- Create new alignments between our lives and the forces around us

❧

Gratitude Practice: Take Stock, Open Up Space

For those who live off the land, taking stock is an act of survival. What crops survived the winter and what will we grow this coming year? How much hay do we need for the livestock? How much storage can we make available for fresh harvests? Stock taking is asking, What do I need? What reserves are in my emotional and spiritual granary that I'm grateful for?

A friend of John's, architect and artist Jim Shay, learned this prayer of thanks from his grandfather, Midwestern prairie farmer Leo Shay, which the family recites on holidays and special occasions: "Dear Father, we thank thee for all the comforts and blessings of life. Help us to receive them with gratitude and to be faithful in our daily duties." Such an elegant, simple prayer is a perfect contract for taking stock. What are our comforts and blessings of life? Our dwelling place—be it walk-up apartment or vast estate—is a good place to begin taking stock. What do we truly treasure? Do the things we really care about stand out from the accumulated clutter? Here's a straightforward exercise for taking stock:

1. Start with a room that feels overcrowded with stuff: stacks of books and magazines, small decorative objects, souvenirs from a recent trip, cards, pictures, and so forth.
2. Remove everything and put the small items in marked boxes.
3. Live the week with the nude room (leave any essentials, such as chairs).
4. Clean, paint, and change window coverings, if needed.
5. Gradually reintroduce the collection of objects into the room, after asking yourself what each item really means to you and others and how can it be most appreciated.
6. Observe the reactions of friends and family.

Dottie, who gave us this exercise, reported that after she'd taken these steps, an old friend came to visit and on entering the room remarked how much she liked the new paintings. But the paintings had been there all along—though poorly lit and hung, surrounded by distracting stuff. Now the space is transformed. What matters to Dottie stands out.

This concept can be applied to the way we will fill our minds and spirits. Is it time for you to take stock? What might be obscuring your view of what is most important to you? For what and to whom do you feel grateful? How could you open up space to let in fresh thinking?

We may find ourselves unexpectedly resistant to doing this work. Who knows what we might find? Wouldn't it be better to just leave things alone? "This is just the way I am," we assert, fearing to let the light penetrate our most secret chambers. Hoarding can be a problem in both our outer and inner homes; usually it is rooted in insecurities. Pack rats are often worried about finances: "I'll never have enough resources if I get rid of any possession, no matter how worn, useless, or superfluous." To calm fears and ease the difficulty, hoarders need to remind themselves that resources now hidden will emerge in the course of letting go of stuff.

Home organizing experts agree that the best approach to dealing with clutter, whether to prepare for a move, downsizing, or clearing out space in your home—and life—is to take it slowly and in stages. Don't try to do it all in one day, and give yourself breaks along the way. The stuff wasn't all accumulated at once, so expect getting rid of it to take some time.

Gratitude Practice: Find Lost Treasures

Done well, spring cleaning should cover every room from basement to attic. A remarkable feature of this dusty trek through closets and cupboards can be the discovery of lost treasures: for example, a favorite shirt you thought was lost hidden at the bottom of a drawer. Another common find is old photographs, sometimes whole albums that force you to stop and reminisce. Such reveries will leave you grateful for the gifts of people from your past.

A priceless life skill is the ability to discriminate between what really matters and what doesn't. Most of the time we do this work automatically, unconsciously. While driving a car, we must decide block by block what signs apply to us: is the child on the bike ahead under control, are the street numbers getting larger or smaller? Searching our interior life for lost treasure calls for even greater discernment—for conscious, careful, and respectful consideration. Here are some important sources of life's "keepers," treasures that can become our touchstones:

- Memories of treasured people who are no longer physically with us but who live in our hearts.

- Struggles that have forced us to learn big, life-altering lessons, and that can guide future decisions. Such struggles include relationships gone sour, ill-conceived schemes gone south, dreams truncated by fear that should have been chased a bit further. Our future learning depends on recalling and using these lessons.
- Talents put aside like an old violin, at risk of drying up. A valuable talent may never have had a real chance, nipped in the bud by a harsh critique, a dull and uninspiring teacher, or a lack of funds. But that repressed talent still lies within you. Bringing it to life only requires some care and attention.

Gratitude Practice: Create New Alignments

Another friend of ours periodically rearranges her furniture as a form of renewal therapy. She believes in the possibility of finding a new order or alignment that she'll find more pleasing to live with. As noted earlier, the central idea behind the Chinese art of feng shui is to create a harmonious alignment between the dwelling, its surroundings, and energy forces. Spring cleaning opens up possibilities for better alignment between the contents of our lives and the forces of nature. It works similarly in our mind and heart space.

For example, in feng shui practice it is considered unfavorable to spend much time directly below a bright overhead light source, or sleeping underneath a beam, which is said to subtly disturb the sleeper's breathing pattern. Heavy chandeliers above a dining table are thought to be oppressive. Is there an influence in your life comparable to a light that won't go off, making you feel under uncomfortable scrutiny? Or something that poses a constant, if low-key, threat?

Can you imagine how to arrange your life's furniture to minimize or avoid these negative forces? On the positive side, can you think of a way to put a strong wall at your back for protection, or how you might take a graceful, curving, indirect path toward a goal rather than a straight line that invites resistance?

Aspects of our lives that need rearranging from time to time are:

- Vocation or career
- Allocation of time and relationships
- Placement of passion

VOCATION OR CAREER

Career moves are excellent opportunities for spring cleaning. What about your current job has brought great satisfaction or dissatisfaction? How could there be more of one and less of the other? Here is a quick exercise to use when considering a career realignment.

Write down the aspects of all previous jobs that brought you pleasure, satisfaction, and fresh learning. Then make a separate list of the dissatisfiers. Distill each list into three themes, and focus your attention on creating a future career path that best matches the themes of your satisfiers. Put aside the dissatisfiers—they will go away as satisfaction increases. A coach can help convert themes into opportunities for gratitude.

ALLOCATION OF TIME AND RELATIONSHIPS

This is an exercise of consciously shifting attention and time away from activities that demand time but are lacking in joy and satisfaction to those where the opposite equation holds. As one friend put it, "Two hours with my newest grandchild is worth more than a week of business meetings." When you can recognize clear choices, then conscious practice over time will help you establish new alignments.

Start by listing two columns of names and activities, for example:

Highest Satisfaction
- Playing golf with Charlie
- Monday meetings with the team
- Attending parties with my spouse

Lowest Satisfaction
- Attending large cocktail parties
- Playing business golf
- Business travel

Now see how many activities in the "low" column can be eliminated or merged into the "high" column. Focus on increasing time for each high-satisfaction activity. Try out your new reallocation of time for one week. Review your feelings, see where you are stuck, and try again for two weeks. Continue to reallocate until you can determine that the alignments mostly favor satisfaction. Your appreciation of this new order will be heightened by finding ways to express gratitude within it, and to the people you have chosen to spend more time with.

PLACEMENT OF PASSION

Identifying where to locate your passion begins by discovering where incipient growth has been frustrated, where you have become root-bound. Recently John's grandchild took a class in Irish dancing and clearly was smitten. A few classes was all it took to see this embryonic passion take hold; soon she was calling excitedly to report three prizes in school competitions. Would that we adults could be so clear and unfettered in pursuing passions. Alas, there is no simple exercise for this, but clearing away the debris of minor distractions is the first step. Passion, like a houseplant, requires room for roots to develop.

Alan's friend David takes a radical approach: about every seven years he sets off on a passion quest. He pulls up stakes and goes traveling to discover something he wants to devote himself to. One quest resulted in a program to distribute food in drought-stricken Africa; another trip launched an education venture. Most of us will not follow David's peripatetic example, but we can try less dramatic versions.

One approach is to list all the past and present passions you have given up or rarely pursue. Such a list might include fishing, biking, chess, ballroom dancing, playing an instrument, meditation, and so on. Lengthen the list by adding activities that attract you but that you've never tried. Once you have a substantial list, ask a good, honest friend or professional advisor to help assign values and probabilities to each item. How much do I value fly fishing and what's the probability it will become a significant and passionate part of my life? Be tough and honest! This is your future. Eliminate all the low probabilities, then rank the remaining ones. Focus lots of thought and attention on the top two, then pick one to pursue wholeheartedly.

Once you have selected your highest passion, make a true adventure of it. Read about it. Make travel plans around it. Invite loved ones to join you. Find coaches, cohorts, a community of like-impassioned souls. Once you are deeply and satisfyingly engaged in this passion, you can allow other interests from your list to claim some attention. Be sure to take note every day of what gifts your passion brings, and imagine how you might give thanks for them.

Pause for Retreat

A retreat is good preparation for the practices outlined above. We can think of a spring retreat as the spiritual and psychological equivalent of a thorough house cleaning. The main features of a successful retreat are quiet and solitude, allowing your attention to move from room to room, past and present, deep into your interior castle to discover what's there. If you can give your mind this space, the treasures of memory, the demons of fear, the unanswered questions, the set-aside loves and talents will surface for you to capture and use.

Just as in a literal house cleaning, you must first remove the clutter—the noise, distractions, and buzzing unconscious desires—so that the hidden treasures stand clear, inviting grateful appreciation. You don't need to go somewhere special, though that is possible. Just find a quiet place in your house or garden, or take a peaceful walk, to create a daily retreat, a time for reflection.

Bless the House

If you have put serious energy into your spring cleaning—of the home, the soul, or both—it should be acknowledged and celebrated. Take time to enjoy the fruits of your labor, bless the results, and thank those who may have helped you. The ritual of a house blessing is available in many religions: you can ask a clergyperson to offer prayers for health and happiness in the home, perhaps burn incense or sage, invite friends to feast and dance, adding whatever personal elements you choose. The secular housewarming party is traditional after a move or a major remodel, but why not throw a spring cleaning party to reward your work of taking stock and opening up, letting in light and air?

If you are celebrating the reopening of your inner house, a private ritual of thanks might be in order, or a dinner party with intimate friends and family. A gently guided conversation could take off from your gratitude for discoveries you have made in the process.

Yard sales and donations, an important part of physical house cleaning, can have their metaphorical equivalents. What do you no longer need to possess that someone else might use? What should you be giving away?

Finally, it can be very useful to get away from your home and normal life from time to time—especially after a period of concentrated focus on these containers of "you"—to get a different perspective. The process of going away and returning, as we all know, can intensify grateful appreciation for the life and home we have built, poured our love and sweat into, and continually seek ways to improve. And remember: in your mind, spring can come at any time.

PART II

Summer

The Flowering of Thanks

When she returned from her annual summer pilgrimage to Cape Cod last year, Alice told us about one day—one hour of one evening, actually—that dwelled in her heart from that busy, happy time:

It was about six P.M., the tide was coming but still pretty low, and we decided to go out on the water. It was such a perfect evening—incredibly clear, with that golden-rose late summer light. Jim got the canoe floating and I went to climb in the bow, but I missed my footing in the reeds and sank up to one knee in the goo. God, did it stink! Well, we finally stopped laughing enough so I could crawl into the boat and rinse off, then we started paddling around the inlet.

We went up the main branch a ways and waved at the fishermen heading in, and marveled at how the pilot got that big, elegant Bahamas yacht into the channel. Then we poked around some tidal creeks and salt ponds so small that we'd never been in them before. The lovely light was draining from the sky, so slowly, and the views became very graphic: still water, a line of reeds with the tide halfway up their stalks, and above that the undulating profile of trees meeting the sky.

The big blue heron we sometimes saw in the mornings took off from our side of the river and we found him again on the other side, plucking mussels from the bank and knocking them on rocks. Other than that and a few late songbirds, it was so very still. My heart almost hurt with thankfulness.

Summer seems to bring an intensification of feeling that probably is linked with childhood memories. Who doesn't remember the wild joy of liberation on the last day of school in June? Or the smells and sounds of a much-loved vacation spot? Our bodies respond to the season's warmth: we shed clothes and, sometimes, cares; we make love without the impediments of nightclothes and bedcovers.

As adults, we're prone to lose or muffle some of the intensity of childhood feelings, but summer is a time when passions can be revived, interrogated, and celebrated; a time to pay attention, especially to the young; a time of refreshment and renewal; a time to give thanks for being alive. Summer is for the opening of closed hearts.

In this season of the book we'll take the next steps past the wonder of springtime rebirth, and explore our grateful responses to life's richness and variety—to the garden in full bloom. Summer's passion has something of heartbreak in it as well as beauty, as in a tender summer evening described by F. Scott Fitzgerald, or C. S. Lewis's concept of "joy" as an intense longing for exaltation.

We'll explore the challenge of finding gratitude and transformation through play, in the way our bodies move and love and labor; through experience that comes through our senses (and how to sharpen appreciation along with the senses); even the path to gratitude that goes through painful experiences. We'll talk about the passionate gratitude inspired by (and required by) the creative arts. And meditate on rest and renewal, the sweet reward of our summertime work and play.

6

Cultivating Gardens
of Gratitude

It is only when you start a garden . . . that you realize something
important happens every day.

      —GEOFFREY B. CHARLESWORTH

A nyone who has ever stuck a seedling in the ground and watched it
grow has experienced the shock of wonder that is the root of all
gratitude. For the child planting a carrot or the master gardener propa-
gating a rare species, there is the same sense of witnessing a miracle,
receiving a gift, participating in a rite as old as time. We are the species
that advanced from hunting and gathering to cultivating our own food,
and later began collaborating with soil, sun, and water to create places
of beauty. Dedicated gardeners have an imperishable source of gratitude always before them—and understand that it remains fruitful only
through faithful tending.

  Gardening is a booming activity today, with a vast public appetite
for books, magazines, catalogs, garden journals, websites, and retail
stores. Some attribute this, like the general surge of interest in home
improvement, to a retreat into private life in threatening times, the
cocooning urge. True enough, but we think people are also responding
to a persistent "inner gardener" who can be satisfied with no substitute
diversions. We are not that far distant in our genetic programming
from our soil-working ancestors; our primal instinct to grow things is
alive and well.

  This is not a chapter just for gardeners. Although we believe any
gardening efforts you make will enrich your gratitude practice, the

history and language of cultivation are so rich in useful metaphor that we can talk about gardens of gratitude even if you never literally put trowel to soil. From the biblical Garden of Eden to Hamlet's image of life as "an unweeded garden that grows to seed" to Voltaire advising us to "cultiver votre jardin" (tend your own garden), poets, prophets, and sermon-writers have plowed, planted, hoed, and fertilized their plots of metaphor to harvest lessons about the virtues of patient toil and abiding faith. People have forever been urged to cultivate their souls, judiciously prune away vices, and so on.

Taking their example, we'll use gardening metaphors in a slightly different way. We've spoken from the start about "cultivating" a gratitude practice, implying a long-term commitment, seasonal rhythms, a learning and growing process that involves a certain amount of sweat. Gardening for gratitude is about creating a place of beauty, peace, fertility, and usefulness within our hearts.

We also want you to think about actual gardens and how they have served humans spiritually—as places where we encounter natural wonders and challenges, as sources of food and healing, as refuges and meditation sites, as places to work out problems and build community. All these functions of the garden help to engender and express gratitude. And think about the qualities that make a good gardener: discernment, imagination, patience, humility, tolerance tempered with rigor. In what ways, including but not limited to actual gardening, can we cultivate these qualities in our lives?

Gardens of Sustenance

Growing plants for food is one of the most basic human acts, imbued with myth, tradition, and rituals of thanksgiving—an act both specific to place and universal. The uses of land, patterns of settlements, and organization of cultures were for millennia grounded in agriculture; millions of people still spend most of their waking hours engaged in growing their own food. It's only in the past century that things have been different for us in the "developed" world, and writers such as Wendell Berry have spoken eloquently about the spiritual disconnect we suffer when our lives become too distanced from our sources of sustenance.

Gardening with vegetables and other edibles has been making a comeback in response to this deeply felt need to connect with the gifts of the soil. Other factors include concern about pesticides in food and the tastelessness of most commercial produce, and rising sophistication in this country about food generally. For most of us, growing a few tomato plants or kitchen herbs is more of a symbolic gesture than a primary source of nutrition. But it's an important act nonetheless. Our city-dwelling friend Dana tried to explain why:

> The garden connects me with so many things, I realize. First of all, there's this powerful seasonal urge; along toward late winter I start to think about the garden again, watching the sun day by day take a higher path so it eventually clears the surrounding buildings and falls on our north-facing yard. Wanting to get out there and turn over the beds, smell earth after the dead season.
>
> It challenges me to be faithful—I tend to start things and abandon them, which you can't do with a garden. Planning what I'll put in makes me draw on my past learning of what has worked or hasn't, connects me with the wisdom of more experienced gardeners whose advice I read, and neighbors who share my microclimate and soil.
>
> When I'm out there, I'm in the middle of a little urban habitat: What do I do about bugs and snails and gophers? Will I get some figs before the birds do? How can I entice more butterflies to visit? The physical labor in just my two four-by-eight beds makes my back ache, and I think in awe of people who work in farm fields all their lives.
>
> Of course, eating our own veggies is really satisfying and yummy. We get enough tomatoes so I only have to buy a few from the farmers' market in August and September—but I also realize the garden provides such a small portion of what we eat. We're so reliant on others raising food for us.
>
> And then there are endless surprises and mysteries. Why did the same kind of beans that did so well last year turn into leafless sticks this summer? Where did those pumpkins and winter squash come from, when I only planted zucchini and crookneck?

All these things, Dana says, provoke feelings of gratefulness and pleasure. Even the frustrations. "I feel engaged in the garden," she says. "As if I can take a hand in helping to create a healthy and happy world—that I can have a working partnership with the physical earth and, if push came to shove, even survive on what I can grow. I don't know if that awareness helps relieve stress . . . but I know that worries seem to drain away when I'm out there."

What are some gratitude principles in Dana's story that can be practiced in or out of the garden? They might include openness to new learning, the rewards of physical labor, observing and working with other species, sharing experience with fellow gardeners. Recognizing one's limits. Pursuing endeavors that bring us face to face with mystery.

The Pleasure Garden

[I]n setting a garden we are painting—a picture of hundreds of feet
or yards instead of so many inches, painted with living flowers and
seen by open daylight—so that to paint it rightly is a debt that we
owe to the beauty of flowers and to the light of the sun.
                                        —WILLIAM ROBINSON, 1883

In a low moment in October, Alan goes out and buys bulbs—daffodils, hyacinths, crocuses, and tulips. Why? Because he remembers that's what he learned to do as a child. He remembers the pleasure of watching them grow and flower indoors during the darkest time of the year, and outside in the garden once the ground began to warm in spring.

No one knows when a human first thought to plant a flowering shrub at the cave entrance or coax a flower into bloom for the sheer enjoyment of it. But the urge to create beauty is sublimely human, and so our efforts to reproduce or improve on nature's beauties were inevitable. "Gardens," says horticulture maven Penelope Hobhouse, "are the result of collaboration between art and nature." A garden is the space where human beings have interfered with, and cooperated with, nature. Some would go further, like garden editor Deborah Needleman, who describes the garden as "ultimately a folly whose goal is to provide delight." In this way, gardening for pleasure is like the mystic's understanding of prayer: useless and an act of sheer praise and adoration.

Gardeners and landscape designers have long debated whether gardens should attempt to recreate natural surroundings in their randomness, or aspire to an ideal of beauty and order not found in nature. Tom Stoppard's play *Arcadia* uses the metaphor of landscape gardening to show how human beings play with such variations in our lives. His subtext arises from contending visions of what a garden should be—formal and "against nature" or striving for a natural look while "tidying up" nature here and there. In his terms, a French garden or an English one?

We don't need to take sides, but it's worth looking at where your gardening impulses lead and where you are most likely to discover gratitude in them. Some lives are too tidy—so clipped and trimmed and geometrical as to preclude the possibility of surprise or relaxed informality. Others could do with a bit of tidying up!

The main thing to keep in mind about pleasure gardens is that they are all about joy. Not just in the payoff of gorgeous blooms and well-tended pathways, but in the every stage of planning, creating, and maintaining them. Like all pleasures, it may intensify and fade with the seasons, or as plantings reach maturity, wither and are replaced. No single joyful moment endures for long in a garden, but gratitude is "the heart's memory," as the French say, and can make all pleasures linger.

Weeds and Wonders

> My garden is a balancing act between weeds and wonders.
> —GARDEN WRITER CAROL STOCKER,
> IN THE *BOSTON GLOBE*, JUNE 1901

The Garden of Eden was idyllic and perfect, with the first couple, Adam and Eve, living in harmony with nature. Then came the business with the apple and the discovery that in every garden there is a snake. In thinking about gardens, we have to be prepared for bugs and snakes, for wanton destruction and unwarranted betrayal. There's also the "garden of good and evil"—a place of lush undergrowth that can seduce and suffocate. Drastic pruning is sometimes necessary.

Your approach to gardening will tell you something about yourself and how you look at the world. A friend of Alan's used to say, "There aren't any weeds—just plants growing in the wrong place!" His attitude made all the difference to his gardening, even if his infinite tolerance could be irritating!

There's a story of a man who had an iris garden. He was passionate about it and wanted only the rarest and best irises, so each year he threw out the more common plants. Being an aficionado, he kept his ear to the ground for news of other people passionate about irises. To his surprise he discovered that someone living nearby also had a very fine iris garden. He was mortified to learn that this garden belonged to the man who collected his garbage! Your rejects may be someone else's treasures.

Our decisions about what to keep and what to throw away are often arbitrary. What is a weed? What is a flower? What is mere noise? What is music? Appreciation and gratitude require training, just as the eye and the ear need training to be able to see and hear things we wouldn't otherwise notice.

John saw a bumper sticker recently that said: "Compost happens!" Composting is another useful gardening metaphor—a way of seeing everything that happens to us as a means of growing a better garden. But you must choose to see that all your experience is the stuff of transformation. Our "reasonable" side argues: "It's dangerous out there, and no one can really be trusted. Better play it safe. Close down." The stench of the compost around life's roses can overpower your sense of its nourishing richness. Yet compost feeds those luxuriant blossoms. We need to stop and smell not just the roses but the muck and mess that help the roses grow.

The word "humility" comes from the kind of earth we call *humus*, rich in organic matter. Good gardeners are realists. They know that all things return to the earth. ("Earth to earth, dust to dust, ashes to ashes.") We came from the earth and we're going back to it. As JoAnn Barwick writes, "There's little risk in becoming overly proud of one's garden because by its very nature it is humbling. It has a way of keeping you on your knees."

The Secret Garden

I do not understand how anyone can live without one small
place of enchantment to turn to.
— NOVELIST MARJORIE KINNAN RAWLINGS

In *The Secret Garden,* the famous 1911 novel by Frances Hodgson
Burnett, an orphaned girl is virtually imprisoned in her uncle's gloomy
mansion on the Yorkshire moors, but finds her salvation (and ultimately that of her family) in a garden that had been kept hidden and
locked away out of grief.

We like the image of a secret garden—a place of refuge and safety
and privacy; a space for renewal, dreams, and fantasies. The soul
needs such a place from time to time. Gardens need protection, so
gardeners know about boundaries and the importance of walls. It's not
that gardeners are grinches; they also know the generosity of nature's
cycles. But they appreciate that a garden sometimes guards the soul.

Alan's friend June seemed like a perfect example of Supermom:
successful career, beautiful kids, great house, designer kitchen with
all the latest gourmet gear. On the surface she was all grace and
charm; inside, she felt pushed to the limit. One afternoon, she told
him, she poured herself what was left of a very good Chardonnay,
walked past the children at play into her garden, and there, for a
moment, a memory came rushing back of what her life had been long
ago, as a child who could hide in a garden.

The garden of her childhood was more unruly than the carefully
laid out one in her present home. Going back in time, she saw a small
girl hiding behind a holly bush that was just thick enough to offer protection from intruders. That was her hiding place—her secret retreat
from family storms. Tears came to her eyes, she confessed over the
phone, because that place of wonder and safety was no longer available to her.

June wanted to recapture the amazement and awe that small people
feel, whether for a Sesame Street creature or a remarkable new flower
that suddenly appears early one morning. Without knowing it, she had
taken the first step towards creating her own garden of gratitude.

Your secret garden is a place where you can always go to become
familiar with your own longing without being terrorized by it. Here you

can be truly at home with yourself, and when that has sunk in, you can be at home with others and in the world. How could you create a safe environment where you can face the truth about yourself without being crushed by what you see, and come out with some hope? Could you make promises in that safe haven to live gratefully, openly, creatively?

Gardens and Community

Voltaire's famous admonition was to "cultiver votre jardin"—cultivate your own garden. One way to read this would be "mind your own business!" We celebrate individualism in this country, and it is one of the great contributions to the human project. But individualism run rampant will undermine a fragile social ecology. Nor is it always personally healthy to escape into one's own private world. Marie Antoinette played shepherdess in her garden at Trianon until revolutionary resentment led to her execution.

Private gardens are important as places where we can retreat, but our journey toward wholeness leads us back by the path of community. Villagers often farm in communal plots, and in communities where individual farms are the rule, neighbors often gather for major efforts like harvests or barn raisings.

In cities around America, the phenomenon of community gardens is spreading fast. Vacant, abandoned lots, often crime magnets in the inner city, are reclaimed and transformed by the hard work of neighbors hungry for green space and eager to grow a little food. Such gardens, a kind of grassroots urban renewal, improve the quality of life for all, encourage business and residential development, lower crime rates, bring generations and cultures together, and provide a venue for neighborhood activities.

In New York City a few years back, garden users and nonprofit groups (one of them spearheaded by Bette Midler) united to prevent the city from auctioning off some 100 community gardens to developers. One of those gardeners, Claire Blum of Project Eden in the Rego Park neighborhood of Queens, says, "The garden is a wonderful place where we can enjoy being outdoors with our family and friends— friends that only a short time ago were neighbors we would just see in passing."

"The leeks, raspberries, swiss chard and rose fir potatoes that Catherine Sneed and her inmate gardeners pull from the soil are not merely fruits and vegetables. Rather, they are metaphors for what went wrong in a prisoner's troubled past, lessons about how to live a healthy and honorable life, and proof that love and work make a garden flourish." So wrote a *New York Times* reporter about an unusual 12-acre farm at a jail south of San Francisco, where a prison counselor and horticulturist teaches gardening to county inmates. The food is donated to soup kitchens and other charities.

"The simple process of weeding is a good place to start re-examining a life gone wrong," says Sneed. "The weeds are whatever got in the way. . . ."

The metaphor hits you in the face—cutting away old leaves to make room for fresh growth. "I take these big, giant crack dealers and show them the roses we've cut back. And they say, 'These ain't no roses; these are dead sticks.' So I say: 'You watch these dead sticks. They're just like you; get rid of the dead stuff and the new stuff will grow.'" As a result of Sneed's vision, she saw lives changed—at least for the time her gardeners stayed in the program.

On the Hawaiian island of Oahu, native taro fields are being restored by halting the diversion of water into canals to irrigate sugarcane fields, and at-risk Hawaiian youth are being introduced to the farming traditions of their ancestors.

On a smaller scale, a couple we know cherishes their weekend time together in the backyard garden. As they go about their tasks, separately or together as needed, there's time for questions and issues to be raised, to remember and relate bits of news from the week that might otherwise go unshared, to plan and fantasize about goals for their home and their lives. Underlying this activity is the reassuring sense of continuity a garden provides, the backdrop of knowing that, whatever is happening today, the plants will come up, the weeds must be pulled, the seasons will change.

Any time you put energy into cultivating a healthy community, you're planting a garden. And the literal act of gardening carries a powerful, hopeful message to those whose relationship with the community has been damaged.

Mind Gardening

Connection with gardens, even small ones, even potted plants, can become windows to the inner life. The simple act of stopping and looking at the beauty around us can be prayer.
— PATRICIA R. BARRETT, *THE SACRED GARDEN*

There are gardens reflecting every side of the human character. There are formal gardens that announce to the world that their owners are people of means and power, able to bend nature to their will in the service of beauty. There are gardens that express a yearning to lose oneself in a deep, mysterious forest, or to be soothed by the sound of running water. There are quirky, personal gardens that display the owner's love of humor and surprise. There are dinky plots of gravel and neglected shrubs that say, "I have no time to pay attention to my surroundings." There are golf courses, vineyards, and Zen gardens of sand and stone.

In thinking of your life and mind as gardens to be cultivated, the first step is discerning what you need to do with your garden at a particular time—a skill that calls for faithful practice. Here are some questions to ask: What work of preparation is needed? Are you, right now, sleeping through a long winter when you need to be preparing for spring? Or is it summer, and is your task to accept the fact that all your hard work is about to pay off, your beautiful garden about to burst into fruit? (With whom will you share your harvest?) Are you in a fall period, when you could use some help in clearing out the summer stalks and preparing the ground for winter frost and spring planting?

All mind gardeners have limited skills and great longings. All have fears that can get in the way of cultivating a garden that can flourish, blossom, bear fruit, and be enjoyed. Perhaps the first rule of mind gardening is to remove the things that make working in the garden sheer hell. Get rid of expectations. Start with plants that are hard to kill, ones you know you can tend.

Remember that each life has its rhythm of engagement and withdrawal. You shouldn't expect to be at "full moon" all the time. Sometimes your life needs to be on the wane. Once you know that, you can stop dumping on yourself when you are at the bottom of the cycle. Allow yourself to lie fallow. The cycle of death and resurrection tells us the earth is getting ready for new birth. In St. John's Gospel we read, "Very truly, I tell you, unless a grain of wheat falls into the earth and dies, it remains just a single grain; but if it dies, it bears much fruit." The same idea and the same delight in gardens is found in all religious traditions.

Martin Luther had the right attitude. He was supposed to have said, "If I knew the world was going to end tomorrow, I'd plant an apple tree today." He was a gardener, one who said, "Thank you!" and got to work.

Gratitude Practice: Gardening and Mind Gardening

1. What kind of garden would you design, if time and resources weren't an issue? A secret garden, a wild garden, a food garden? A garden to attract birds, or to experiment with colors? What could you do, given your current resources and level of skill, to begin such a garden? Or to create a symbolic version of it? How would such a garden serve your gratitude practice?

2. Ask yourself, the mind gardener, these questions: Where are you in your own life cycle at this moment? Are you in your garden alone? Whom would you like (or not like) to have in the garden with you? Do you have a community? What time is it seasonally? Is it getting cold, are you afraid? Do you have a coat on? Are the walls too close? Do you feel confined in this garden? Is it overgrown, too lush? Does it need pruning? Has it been watered lately? Where is the garden threatened, from within or without? Is it bugs, or neglect? Do you know where true north is? Do you feel at home here?

These are only a few of many possible questions. With some practice in the language of cultivation, you can think of the best ones to ask yourself. What are you most grateful for in this garden of your mind?

7

Thanking Our Dragons

Perhaps all the dragons in our lives are princesses who are only
waiting to see us act, just once, with beauty and courage.
—RAINER MARIA RILKE

The Dragons of Summer

In spring we began our journey through the seasons of gratitude by looking at life's more obvious blessings: the wonders of creation, the natural
world, family life, our homes and gardens. In summer we need to
expand and deepen our gratitude practice to encompass other aspects
of life—the terrifying dragons along with the beautiful princesses. We
take on the challenge of finding gratitude and transformation in
painful experiences or difficult relationships. In this way your gratitude practice can unfold into full summer bloom.

Those dragons—some of them societal or global, others purely personal—may be princesses only waiting to see us act with beauty and
courage. Gratitude is the charm that can turn a dragon into a princess.
The eternal dragons of time, death, and love have to be faced. They are
the great uncontrollables, the great unfixables. Time cannot be stopped.
Death is inevitable. Love cannot be forced, bought, or commanded.

And death is the biggie—the great dragon to which all the others
are related. We all know we are going to die one day, but there's something in us that doesn't really take this dragon seriously until something comes along to knock us over the head. We lose our job, have an

85

accident, get sick, lose a loved one or a marriage. Life falls apart. But the great religious traditions teach us that a sense of mortality—as it relates to wonder and astonishment—can be the doorway to intense participation in life as a gift. Death becomes the prism through which we see that life is to be lived day by day and with gratitude. The dragon becomes a friend. But how can this happen?

In another poem, "The Man Watching," Rilke shows us the futility of trying to shut down life as if life were our enemy.

> What we choose to fight is so tiny!
> What fights with us is so great!
> If only we would let ourselves be dominated
> as things do by some immense storm,
> we would become strong, too, and not need names. . . .
>
> When we win it's with small things,
> and the triumph itself makes us small. . . .
> Winning does not tempt that man.
> This is how he grows: by being defeated decisively
> by constantly greater beings.

For some, life is a constant battle where people stab each other in the back, often for very low stakes. Our winnings are puny and our victories empty. Rilke is challenging us with something profound and important. There is an energy in the universe that is ultimately on our side. We grow by surrender. We deepen by letting ourselves go, by not trying to fix the unfixables of time, love, and (above all) death.

This concept of giving over is much easier to describe than to live, especially when life seems a huge struggle and even small victories are hard to find. It may be why some people cannot really enjoy time off. Summer, traditionally, is a time to slow down and take a break. But that's hard for type A personalities, those addicted to velocity. Frankly, some of us hate summer. Vacations threaten us. The last thing we want to do is to slow down and have time to make choices.

The trouble with letting the lid off is that stuff lurking beneath the surface of our lives tends to bubble up uninvited. The dragons come out to play. We might be persuaded to take a weekend off as long we have our cell phone, but to take a good chunk of time off is unthinkable. Lying on the beach or simply hanging around invites deep questions that we'd rather avoid to stroll up and introduce themselves.

This problem, traditionally associated with men, is as much an issue for women these days. Believing that we have no time is a comforting illusion for those addicted to velocity. If the truth were told, summer, with its promise of relaxation, comes as a threat. We daren't take our foot off the pedal—who knows where life might take us.

Your Long-Term Strategy

Alan:

> A cartoon came across my desk. Shared with John, it raised smiles because we both struggle with lives that are too full. Sometimes it's hard to tell the difference between doing a good job and having a tight grip on everything. We're frightened that we might miss something. The cartoon depicted a man proudly showing his boss an impressive chart. The caption read: ". . . and our *ultra* long-term strategy will be to burn up when the sun becomes a red giant."

What is your ultra long-term strategy? What are you working *for*? Type A personalities get impatient with ultimate questions. They think that nothing, in principle, is unfixable or unanswerable. Some things are better left unasked. Nevertheless, when we slow down, unbidden thoughts and feelings creep into our consciousness. Why are we here? What is life about? Who am I? Who are you? Who cares?

Death has to be part of our long-term strategy if don't want that dragon to scare us into a living grave. We two are of an age that, with a group of men of a certain age, the subject of prostate cancer inevitably comes up. One of our friends calls it the "organ recital!" Most men die with it if not of it. And there's not simply one way to treat it. Some men can't stand the thought of having cancer inside them so they say, "Cut the sucker out." Sometimes that's a good way to go; sometimes the results aren't good. Likewise for other responses: various forms of radiation, hormone treatment, diet, and so on.

The point is that many men are being introduced, perhaps a little earlier than usual, to the dragon of mortality. A friend of ours has noticed that ever since his diagnosis he's been much nicer to people. He made a choice to be grateful for the gift of life.

Dragons in the World

Just as individuals have their dragons to confront and transform into something positive—into bearers of life—so do nations and cultures. Our personal dragons have implications for society. We are an anxious and depressed society in many ways, partly due to our inability to look what we dread in the eye. The presence of so many desperate souls in our midst can cause a paralyzing anxiety in the most stable and optimistic of us. These fears roam our streets and surface in international relations, making enemies of neighbors and devils of entire populations or religious groups.

Since September 11, 2001, we now dread terrorism more than ever. If we are not careful, we will turn everyone we meet into a potential enemy. "Will this person hurt me? Does that one wish me harm?" If we let them, the dragons in the world and on our streets will migrate off the TV screen and invade our private lives.

According to philosopher Jim Carse, the Sufis speak of their *nafs,* a false sense of self that can take the place of the soul. This persona is another kind of dragon—the mask we wear in front of others. We get into trouble when we forget that it is a mask and wear it for too long. The nafs has a life of its own: logical, powerful, real. The Sufis describe it as a hungry yellow dog that always stands begging at our side. For some of us, the first step on the road to freedom is to face that hungry yellow dog and send him on his way.

Back during the dot-com boom, we both took part in a discussion with a group of people in business—some who had made a lot of money and others who hoped for an IPO to vault them to the top. There was a lot of energy and creativity in the room, but what struck us was the objectified view these people had of reality. They took for granted that the world was a kind of base material for them to play with. They saw it as an unsafe and inhospitable place, but also as a theater for their exploitation and delight. Globalization, to them, was not an invitation to greater community but a license to look after number one and carve out their own piece of paradise.

But this stance of objectifying the world and isolating themselves had gotten these business leaders into trouble. Some were growing aware that distrust had become their preferred strategy for running not just their businesses but their lives—with serious consequences for family and working relationships. They knew enough to know it didn't feel right. They didn't yet know that in trying to set themselves apart, they risked making their home in a virtual world—a sure step toward death in life. They didn't know that the dragons were waiting for them.

Your Personal Dragons

Early one morning last summer, Pat was sitting in her study wondering how she came to be the way she was—over fifty, just over a cancer scare, divorced after twenty-five years, the kids all out of the nest. She was puzzled. "I've never been happier or felt better," she said to herself. She didn't expect to be so content in spite of the guilt and shame at failing in marriage and the constant reminder of mortality. Dragons: cancer, divorce, and failure. She looked them all in the eye and found new life in living gratefully.

Over that early morning cup of coffee, Pat learned one of the lessons of summer—compassion for herself. One key to the palace of gratitude is forgiveness. To judge is to come to an end. To forgive is to start again.

Pat later wrote a poem to help understand what had happened to her. It's called "Dragons," after Rilke's famous reference to dragons turning into princesses, and it incorporates the wounds of both cancer and lost love.

When Pat wrote the poem, she realized that her life wasn't over after all. The shift in her consciousness was anticipated by two things. First, her body demanded attention and she followed its lead: she ate more healthily, got more exercise, lost weight, and in general felt more at home in her skin. Second, the upheavals in her life and even a growing sense that death is the last great adventure gave her a new voice.

There was an awakening of the poetic imagination, which exactly suited what was happening to her.

That creative work can arise from the struggle with one's dragons is a common thread in the lives of many artists. To give just one example, the novelist W. Somerset Maugham said, "What has influenced my life more than any other single thing has been my stammer. Had I not stammered I would probably [not have become a novelist but] gone to Cambridge as my brothers did, perhaps have become a don and every now and then published a dreary book about French literature."

The Cancer Dragon

Alan:

I am taking part in a scientific study (under the direction of the cardiologist Dean Ornish) with a great group of men. We have undertaken a strict regime of diet and lifestyle change to see if prostate cancer can be arrested or even eliminated. A friend in the study said to me the other day, "I now realize I applied to take part in this study not so much to cure my cancer as to open my heart. And this is what's happened. I would never have had this opening into new life if I hadn't had this cancer scare."

The dragon turned out to be a princess. I have to admit this makes me a bit nervous, and I want to be careful how I speak of it. I have never felt as fit as I do now under this regime of diet, exercise, yoga (they call it stress management), and group support. But I still wish I didn't have cancer. Long before I knew of my diagnosis, in a conversation over dinner at a conference, my companion not only told me that he had cancer but that he wished I had it too because having it had changed his life. I wanted to hit him. I can now see something of what he meant but it still strikes me as a stupid thing to say. What is wonderful is everything in my life that is *not* the disease; this dragon is only a princess for helping me see that.

What have I learned? Mainly to make and keep appointments with myself. You might try this. Go through your calendar and make dates with yourself. Try blocking out whole days. When someone wants to see you, say, "Sorry, but I have an appointment." You don't have to tell them it's with yourself. You will give yourself the gift of time—time to allow the scattered bits and pieces of your life to come back together. The dragons will still be there but they will begin to change as you give them your attention. I call this exercise "Getting to know my dragons."

Another thing I've learned is to treat my body differently—as beloved friend, not something I *have* but something I *am*. The prostate study requires that I do an hour a day of meditation, breathing, yoga, and relaxation. I would never have taken on this regime without the incentive of the study, but it is now part of my routine. It doesn't take away my struggles with life but it does put them in a different place, and (I don't know how to put it another way) when I encounter the dragons I encounter them in a more secure place inside me. They are not quite princesses yet, but I'm in a position to allow for the possibility. It's as if when the body is honored, the psyche is refreshed and strengthened. You might try a modest routine of this sort—even better is finding someone to do it with.

Gratitude Practice: Really Look at Your Dragons

What we learn through experience is that when we take time to really look at something, we change for the better. Take the dragon of an anxious and resentful mood on a bright summer day. You look out of the window and see a tree in full leaf. You take time to look at it, really look at it. *In a moment everything is altered.* The tree has your attention, and for that moment anxiety and resentment disappear, and a sense of wonder and gratitude takes their place.

This simple practice is available to us all the time. It just takes remembering. The world is always offering itself to us in this way. If we look at a tree, a flower, almost anything with a receptive eye, our mind begins to operate from a different and deeper place.

Sometimes these small acts of contemplation make demands on us. In order to complete the transformation of the dragon, we have to offer a grateful response. You might be prompted to make that phone call, write that letter, plan that visit to say "Thank you!" or "Sorry!" or "I love you!"

Summer is a good time for such practices because everything is in full bloom and vibrant with life, and at the same time we know that the year's decay is just around the corner. In the long days and evenings, we have time to look at the big questions and, knowing everything comes to an end, truly learn to enjoy the world.

It's time to take a look at what has died in your life. The naïveté and enthusiasm of youth? The love of a life long past? A view of your native land that you no longer believe in? W. H. Auden in one of his poems suggests that, "we would rather be ruined than changed. We would rather die in our dread than climb the cross of the moment and see our illusions die." If we are unwilling to stop and look, the dragons not only remain incapable of transformation, they gain in power.

Remember Rilke's words: We grow "by being defeated decisively by constantly greater beings." Thanking our dragons is a way of allowing those greater beings to come to life in us.

8

Playing Live

The most powerful agent of growth and transformation is something
much more basic than any technique: a change of heart.

— JOHN WELWOOD

For most of us, summer vacations are a time to reconnect with our
bodies and recapture the exuberance of youth, to be temporarily
carefree. The rest of the year we may use our bodies as a transport system to carry around our brains and laptops. We become numb tired,
mindless, focused on work; we hunch, overeat and overdrink, swallow
stress, develop guts, and wonder why our backs hurt and our stomachs
rebel. We plan holiday escapes to exotic places and dream of one day
being financially free so we can play nonstop. But when our annual
holiday comes, our expectations often exceed the experience and we
come back sore, sunburned, and strangely out of sorts.

Ask the modern parents of small to high-school-age kids how they
plan to spend the summer, and they will describe a wide range of
camps, sports leagues, and events that require drivers. And of course
the parents will have their own plans for hiking, biking, tennis, golfing,
scuba diving, rafting, and so on. All these activities can be classified as
play, but are they truly playful or just a different form of serious striving? Or even just time fillers?

We believe there's a vast difference between play that's approached
as a task, a rehearsal, or a contest, and what we'll call "playing live." Playing live is about joyous spontaneity, improvising, enjoying, learning as
we go. It's about losing oneself in the moment, in the delight-filled,

liberating, soul-stretching, wholly absorbing exercise of body, mind, or both at once. It is not tediously constrained and harshly self-critical. Playing live can be blissfully joyous, a way of gratefully celebrating life itself.

Looking at how children play is the best place to start thinking about playing live. Children get lost in their play, lose track of time, forget where they are. They completely enter into the parts they play; when they play doctor they do it with conviction. Yelps of laughter come easily: a wet dog can send them into spasms. They are curious about the most minute objects, peering riveted into tidepools and ant colonies. They cherish things without regard for their market value: old blankets, broken dolls, faulty cats, plain goldfish.

As we grow up, where does that playful spirit go? We are told to grow up, put away childish ways. Teenagers often give up childish play as a way of emulating their serious parents. Play becomes more and more competitive and regimented. Acting like a kid isn't cool. Some report feeling dead inside and may turn to drugs and booze to feel alive. By the time we reach adulthood, we may have so distanced ourselves from playing live that we've made play into a form of work.

When we lose the capacity to lose ourselves in play, we are less fully alive. Even children who suffer traumas can stop playing or play with a joyless seriousness like adults. A powerful executive that John once counseled describes what happened to him:

> Saturday golf was supposed to be my relaxation formula. On the golf course I thought I could get involved and forget business. However, I began to notice something that told me it wasn't working very well. I became aware that the three guys I played with had started to walk down the other side of the fairway from me. When I asked one of them why this was happening, he told me that my anger was driving them away. After getting angry about what he said, I realized that my anger was out of control. Maybe all the stuff I couldn't blow up about at work was getting hauled onto the golf course. Golf became a time for venting rather than just having fun and relaxing.

Golf is a game that can never be mastered, some say. Certainly it can be pursued either as play or as deadly serious and frustrating work. It can bring out the kid or the achievement monster in us. Playing can be a lovely, challenging walk with friends or a dangerous maze of self-imposed torture. Golf courses are the most likely places for middle-aged Japanese executives to have a heart attack—that's serious.

How You Play the Game

We know instinctively that we need play in our lives, and studies of both animals and humans back up that sense. Play has a key role in physical, emotional, and social development, but experts believe that the chief purpose of play is simply pleasure.

For our own species, the play of healthy, secure, loved children is the best model we have of pure play—play that makes us feel keenly alive, that evokes gratitude. The problem lies in another powerful human trait: our drive to organize and regularize. It's a paradox that in developing ever more complex, organized forms of play, we have risked losing its essential spirit.

But the subversive, explosive spirit of play is hard to kill off entirely. Aside from sheer, jaw-dropping appreciation of athletic talent, this is what keeps us watching professional sports. Catch the little-boy grin of superstar Barry Bonds, subject of so much controversy, as he swats a landmark home run in a big game. Watch the victorious World Series team pour off the bench, leaping awkwardly skyward with uncontainable joy as they pile on their teammates on the field.

Start thinking about play in a different way. Novelist and Esalen founder Michael Murphy notes that any form of play, physical or mental, can be a joyous, enlightening experience. It is our choice and our opportunity. A solitary run, a crossword puzzle, a game of charades, or a pick-up soccer game can all be played with a mindful intent, child-like abandon, or both. Playing live can keep us youthful, bring us closer to others, or give us a needed hour of solitude. For all of this we should be grateful.

The universe of opportunities for play is nearly limitless, as we see it. Organized athletics are just one among many galaxies in this cosmos. Other physical pastimes, solitary or social, range from high-altitude mountaineering to snorkeling to romping with the family dog. Card games, board games, word games, and puzzles represent the galaxy of mental play, which can be either highly social or a way to keep the mind lively in private.

Don't stop there. We can use play in so many other parts of our lives. Conversation is where we exercise our wits with others who stimulate our mind, or just succumb to pure silliness with those we most trust. Love play helps keep intimate relationship ever inventive, ever fresh and surprising. Those who can leaven their working life with a dose of playfulness are less likely to suffer from stress on the job and more likely to enjoy beneficial relationships with coworkers. And sometimes our own thoughts lead us on a delightful chase with a surprise ending that can make us laugh out loud even if no one else is around: mind play.

In this context, whether you win or lose isn't especially relevant and we don't even need to debate it. Sometimes it's important, sometimes not. But *how you play the game* is indeed the critical point. Playing in ways that bring us to another level of consciousness, or that restore us to our "animal" state of unconsciousness. (Athletes speak of being in the "zone": a place where time slows down, vision widens and sharpens, decisions flow without thought. This may be the closest we can come to an animal operating on genetically primed instinct.) Play that evokes deep feelings of gratitude.

Deep Play

The Greek ideal of human virtue was *mens sana in corpore sano,* a view that incorporated the play of mind and the physical play. Competition was about achieving personal excellence. Playing live was an everyday thing manifested and celebrated through sporting contests, theater, debate, the arts, and learning generally. We're reminded of a concept articulated by essayist Diane Ackerman, which she calls transcendent play or "deep play." This special dimension of play—"the ecstatic form of play"—is something human beings require in order to feel whole, she believes:

> In its thrall, all the play elements [the delights of silliness, perfecting coordination, rehearsing the rules of courtship and society] are visible, but they're taken to intense and transcendent heights. Thus,

deep play should really be classified by mood, not activity. It testifies to how something happens, not what happens. Games don't guarantee deep play, but some activities are prone to it: art, religion, risk-taking, and some sports—especially those that take place in relatively remote, silent and floaty environments, such as scuba diving, parachuting, hang gliding, mountain climbing.

Here's an even broader scope for the universe of play. It's not hard to see the creative and performing arts as fertile arenas for play. But religion—isn't that serious stuff? "If you look at religious rites and festivals," writes Ackerman, "you'll see all the play elements, and how deep that play can become. Religious rituals usually include dance, worship, music and decoration. They swallow time. They are ecstatic, absorbing, rejuvenating. . . . Deep play always involves the sacred and holy, sometimes hidden in the most unlikely or humble places—amid towering shelves of rock in Nepal; crouched over a print in a dimly lit room; slipping on Astro Turf; wearing a coconut-mask. We spend our lives in pursuit of moments that will allow these altered states to happen."

Another intriguing sense in which to think about deep play is risk taking. Not necessarily the physical kind, but the kind of risk taking with which entrepreneurs and others in the business world are familiar. Approaching this as a form of play could be transforming, and certainly a source of gratitude.

Philanthropists Dick and Lois Gunther aren't content with just giving away money. They want to take a hand personally. Now in their seventies, they recently visited a rural village in remote western China to help set up a microlending program.

"Our small gift was overmatched by their enthusiasm, the deep gratitude each villager expressed," recalls Dick. "Our aches and pains and jet lag went away as we talked with them. Microlending has become a real passion, and this time we'd gone thousands of miles to exercise it. I suppose there might have been an easier way, but it sure felt good."

Playful banking—now there's a concept!

Five Fallacies About Play, and How to Avoid Them

Let's look more closely at the ways we sometimes fail to play live. Gratitude-linked practices can help us avoid these deadening beliefs and habits, and to explore opportunities for deep, satisfying play.

1. Play is separate from the rest of life, and its rewards are limited to a short-term high.

This is an easy trap to fall into, because as adults we tend to think of play as something restricted to our leisure time. And since that time is so rare and precious, we may feel cheated if our play experience doesn't produce the euphoric effect we seek. Even if we do get the exhilaration, a letdown can easily follow, ranging from disappointment to depression.

Top athletes are very aware of this problem, and the wise ones work hard to gain some perspective. After winning his third consecutive Tour de France, Lance Armstrong put it well, saying, "It is very exciting—words can't describe it—but it is also only one phase of my life. I won't be a bike rider forever." Playing live is not a contest or a culminating high moment. It is a process, a day-by-day opportunity.

A friend of John's had to relearn how to live playfully after a lifetime of high-performance moments. Agnes is a 53-year-old former dancer who had her spine fused following a car accident. After a period of mourning the loss of her former athleticism, she created a new life to accommodate the special circumstances of looking down at life at a 45-degree angle.

These days Agnes plays live by learning the piano and riding horses, both activities where her bent posture works fine. "When I first play a piece in the morning I completely forget my back," she says, "and each time I play I liven up. And the minute I'm in the saddle my spirits rise, the pain goes away like magic. I'm grateful for my piano and horses every hour of every day. I used to believe that I was only fully alive when I danced. Now I try to look for that feeling in whatever I'm doing."

Gratitude Practice: Fighting the Temptation to Live Life as a Series of Highs

- Identify an activity you can do every day that brings you satisfaction and joy. Examples are cooking, gardening, singing, walking, reading aloud, playing a game, and reading.
- Work in regular time (make an appointment with yourself) to pursue this activity as play.
- Make notes on the feelings that come from this practice, how the dough feels as you make crust. Does it sometimes start to feel like work? Or, better put, like you're not enjoying it? How could you change the way to approach it so it feels more playful?
- Create a way to express gratitude for this opportunity: it could be a statement, a prayer, or an action, like including someone else.

2. Significant play involves a lot of planning; it doesn't happen spontaneously.

This fallacy arises from the serious aspect play takes on in adulthood, and the way we compartmentalize our lives. Playing live can come out of a preplanned event, but we are just as likely to stumble on a transcendent moment by accident. Allowing opportunities for play in our work, for example, can create spontaneous occasions for gratitude.

Anyone who has watched big-time professional golf knows how intense it can become. For the pros, it *is* their work, so it becomes hard to remember that it's just a game. At a time when hard-living pro John Daley was getting a lot of media scrutiny for problems in his personal life (as well as failures in the game), fellow golfer and commentator Jonny Miller wisely commented, "If you [Daley] are having a good time it is important to stop and count your blessings and then resume play." A small, unplanned moment of gratitude can remind us that it is good to be alive, to be playing a game we love in a beautiful place. It may even improve our game.

The great mathematician Albert Einstein spoke of his work as play. For him, the beginning of creativity involved "associative play," which sometimes formed into concepts that could be reproduced.

Gratitude Practice: Expand Your Capacity for Spontaneous Play

- Look for chances to turn life into a festival of unplanned play. A friend likes to turn on his favorite dance music rather loud (like a disco), grab a broom, and dance on his balcony after a long hard day.
- Create small adventures. For example, try varying your routines such as the route you take to work. One executive commutes on his bike, often stopping for a coffee in some new neighborhood where he meets new people. He says he arrives at work feeling refreshed.
- Take an unpleasant obligation and turn it into something creative. A woman friend with a chronic illness uses her waiting time in the doctor's office to write small poems and songs to fight off bad vibes. The first was about the waiting room, and she liked it enough to give it to her doctor. After that, he took much more interest in her.

3. Some kinds of play are better than others, more important, more worthy of our time.

Believing that play can be ranked is chilling to the spirit. If your time is too valuable to spend on any kind of play except one that confers social status or leads toward a goal, you are not really playing. The idea that some play is intrinsically more valuable than another is wrong. Yet our yearning for order and significance can lead us into compulsive ways.

Which is more "important": a game of pick-up baseball in a park with friends, or a professionally organized horseback outing? Of course, there is no right answer, for each of us needs to make individual choices about our play. Even putting the words *play* and *important* side by side is to miss the point. Play is only important in concept, not form. One person's play may be another's work.

Gratitude Practice: Keep Play in Perspective

- If you find yourself getting compulsive about play, try to step back and recall why you took up an activity in the first place. Am I golfing for fun or for psychological venting? Why is singing no longer satisfying? When did I decide it had a lower priority than playing serious tennis? Explore what you could do to recapture the joy you once felt in the activity.
- Leave some unstructured free time, on a weekend or whenever you can take it, and choose something you don't usually do for fun. It can be alone or with others. Make note of what happens.
- When the good feelings are flowing—like after your big scene in the amateur play—let them rush in. Don't debate their significance: Is this the highest use of my talent? Shouldn't I be singing on Broadway? Wrong questions. Playing live is what we are doing right now!

4. There are no limits to playing live;
it can be artificially extended at will.

It's a hazardous assumption that more of any good thing will be better. This folly can play out in ways as innocent as savoring chocolate too often or as dangerous as snorting coke a second time. When an aging athlete tries for one more grand season or a tired performer attempts to pump up the audience on sheer adrenaline, it's rarely about play any longer. What was once live and yeasty is suddenly a long march.

Drugs or alcohol are a common way to artificially extend experiences like dancing, listening to music, or sex. A soccer player describes a similar phenomenon in sports: "We got into the habit of hauling our hurting bodies and excited spirits into a pub following our matches. The idea was to keep the game's natural high going with a few pints, some teasing, a song or two. It worked all right for awhile and then the whole thing went wrong. Lads drank too much. Fights broke out and people got hurt. We went too far."

The story speaks for itself about the hazards of play artificially sustained. Playing live occurs in the moment, and that can't be manipulated.

Gratitude Practice: Don't Stretch a Good Thing Too Far

- Develop proper endings for your play and other life experiences.
- Plan a small celebration to mark achievements and honor those who shared them with you.
- Appreciate your victories as fully as possible, but don't brood about repeating them.

5. Play must be organized and measured.

Comparing, keeping score, insisting on rules—the belief that play must include these elements is among the most common adult handicaps. Any child can demonstrate how upside-down it is. Imposing measurements on playing live is driving a stake into the heart of creativity. In fact, anything that makes us too purposeful and self-conscious defeats the free flow of discovery. With too much regimentation, adults may kill the fun not just in their own play but in that of children.

Linda was the epitome of the organized, do-it-well woman. Each day she would dutifully make a list of tasks, and by nightfall they would all be checked off. Her children's activities took up much of her time. One day while racing through her tasks, she dropped her two boys at the soccer practice field early in order to get across town to her next stop. But she had dropped them at the wrong field—a fact she discovered when her cell phone rang an hour and a half later.

Frantically she drove back to find the boys kicking the ball around.

"What happened?" she screamed. "Nothing, we just played," said Bret, the older. "But practice, where was practice?" she insisted. "It's OK, Mom—we practiced a lot," replied Tommy. Linda had forgotten that play can be practice and practice can be play. Happily, she's now in therapy learning about the playful urges that her compulsiveness had throttled.

Gratitude Practice: Rescue Fun from the Jaws of Score Keeping

- Give up keeping score for a while. A wise friend plays golf without keeping score, and picks up the ball whenever it doesn't look fun to hit it. She says, "When I play this way, I have so much more fun and I really am grateful for the walk and talk. I only keep track of the shots that really feel good." This sounds like playing live.
- Turn work into play, but never turn play into work. Take risks in favor of playing live.

Whatever your game, don't forget to remind yourself often of why you first loved it, and try for that feeling every time. And consider how you might infuse everything you do with gratitude by approaching it in the spirit of deep play.

9

Living in the
Realm of the Senses

Without the body, the wisdom of the larger self cannot be known.
— John Conger

❧

Summer is a time of a wondrous sensuality—life in full bloom. It's the time for farmers' markets with summer fruits: luscious peaches, nectarines, berries, plums, figs. And the vegetables! Beans, peas, zucchini, peppers, and corn. And fantastic tomatoes, with thin skin and real taste. Summer is a festival for the senses. The season invites us to develop a zest for life and a taste for the real and earthy. This appetite for sensate life can be described with the Spanish word *gusto* (taste). And from another word for "taste"—the Latin *sapere*—comes a kind of wisdom, *sapientia*.

We experience the world through our senses, which give evidence both that we are alive and that one day we will die. Evolution has bestowed on us a well-rounded array of sensing apparatus that is among the greatest gifts of being human. Nearly everything that can inspire gratitude comes to us courtesy of the senses: visual beauty, transporting music, scents that soothe or stir memories, delectable tastes, pleasurable caresses. The "thank you" we breathe when another's touch brings the gift of sexual ecstasy is among our most heartfelt. Even when the information that comes via our senses isn't pleasurable, it's always useful: the smell of food gone bad, for example, or the pain that signals an injury. We are creatures of flesh.

We may lose our zest for life because we don't feel at home in our bodies—if we're cut off from the realm of the senses. And how do we dare "taste" new things? Shouldn't we be cautious? They might be dangerous, even lethal. We are the beneficiaries of generations of trial and error: our ancestors tried something and concluded that we could or could not eat it. But we can't rely solely on received knowledge. What are we prepared to take in, to taste, discovering what nourishes and what causes pain?

The human organism has to taste ideas, too. Wisdom—*sapientia*—comes from digesting knowledge so thoroughly that it becomes part of us. It is a collaborative adventure within ourselves using all our senses. It means allowing the body to teach us things we cannot learn in any other way.

Don't Be Disembodied

Many of us are like James Joyce's Mr. Duffy who "lived a short distance from his body." In fact, we may live some distance from our bodies, and it can take enormous effort to get back in touch with our five senses. In trying, we often go overboard and get destructive with our bodies or what we put into them. We overindulge, sometimes become addicted, in order to feel alive. The road to recovery lies in learning to love our bodies and to make a direct connection with the world through our senses.

There's a lot of guilt about the body. The English science writer Jeremy Burgess wonders, "Is it just me, or does everyone else feel guilty for being alive too? . . . Eventually, and probably soon, we shall be reduced to creeping about in disgrace, nervous of our simplest pleasures." We suspect that a lot of people feel guilty just by virtue of existing. We might not describe ourselves that way, but functionally many of us struggle with irrational guilt about drawing breath. The temptation to shut down parts of our lives in penance is enormous.

Every day we can choose to be either open or closed to what the philosopher Søren Kierkegaard called "the wounds of possibility." It would be safer to close down but then we risk going dead. Staying open to the wounds of possibility protects us from being frozen in habit and custom. It helps subvert our fears and keep us alive.

When we lose touch with our senses, we become slaves to the dragons of our inner life: fear, guilt, self-pity, hurt feelings, anger, lovesickness. Often this happens as a result of being hurt in an intimate relationship. Maggie, a friend of Alan's wife, recalls the vicious cycle precipitated by a recent breakup.

> When Richard dumped me—of course, he didn't put it that way—I think I just shut down, physically as well as emotionally. I would spend all my waking hours at work, not even going out for air at lunch. When I did go out at night, it was on computer dates where once was always enough—I even slept with a couple of those guys but couldn't get aroused sexually. I was overeating and not really tasting anything. And letting myself slide that way just made my self-respect take an even deeper dive. It took me a long time to get past that stage.

The negative emotions wear us out with relentless repetition. We become fatalistic, trapped in the same old patterns—the betrayals and heartbreaks, the petty crimes and hollow triumphs, the "wrong" kind of man or woman—the same mistakes. We hallucinate reality and live in the consequent distortions. It's an impossible scenario in which to feel grateful.

Two classic distortions get in the way of living fully through the senses. A distorted view of religion sees the body as a distraction to be avoided or suppressed in order to pursue a truly spiritual life. This attitude has wrought havoc with our need for healthy sexual intimacy.

Another distortion isn't so obvious but can be as harmful as repressive religion. Indulgence is a parody of true sensuality, and actually blunts the keenness of our senses. Part of the problem is that living sensually takes time, and we tend to believe that some quick fix or amped-up sensory experience will satisfy our needs. Overeating and substance abuse are the most typical penalties for this thinking; promiscuous sexuality poses stark hazards for others. But we can also indulge to excess in apparently healthy pursuits like exercise or hobbies. Any indulgence that passes for sensuality without giving life the time to touch us is a road to zonked-out oblivion. True sensuality requires being awake and present.

Falling into the Body

Sometimes we are catapulted back into our bodies with a vengeance. It can be pleasant or horrifying. We feel pain in the chest, break a leg, pull a muscle. We miss a step and fall flat on our face. Whatever it is, it brings us down to earth and into the body. Alan's friend, the late Charles Corn, describes such a moment in his book, *Distant Islands: Travels Across Indonesia*. Chuck was attending a funeral, a weeklong ritual at which he was seated among the family members. Imagine a feast for the senses: a procession of exquisitely veiled young women in bejeweled, full-length dresses of saffron and magenta, moving from the death house to a pavilion. He writes:

> In the middle of this solemn processional, I shifted my weight and the legs of my chair slipped through cracks in the makeshift floor with a crash, sending me tumbling over in a back somersault, nearly spilling me into the pig-fouled mud. The entire compound broke out in riotous laughter exempting no one.

He notes that his interruption of this solemn occasion seemed almost welcome. "Pretense was acceptable if it could be brought low by a pratfall from the unexpected. As an outsider, I was the unwilling source."

This has implications for the choreography and drama of everyday life. A unexpected pratfall is sometimes the way our "earthiness" is revealed to us. Jung once spoke of this experience as a pilgrimage back down out of the clouds into our bodies. He writes of having to climb down back to the earth to accept the little clod of earth that he was. This wasn't self-negation but true humility. The monk Thomas Merton records having a similar experience in a crosswalk in Louisville. He jumped for joy when he realized that he was like everybody else— a human being, a creature in solidarity with all creation.

But not everyone jumps for joy at that realization. One reason we may try to ignore the senses or zonk out with excess is that our bodies remind us of our extreme vulnerability. The gift of life can be taken away so suddenly and unexpectedly. Holding this awareness rescues us from the danger of imagining that we are morally self-sufficient or excellent. Celebrating our vulnerability and finitude places our fears and dreads where they belong—not at the center of life but at its edge. We are closer to the mystery at the heart of things, to which the proper response is gratitude.

Celebrate Our Creatureness

Alan got to know the renowned primatologist Jane Goodall when she came to speak at Grace Cathedral. Whether or not she is aware of it, Jane exemplifies a life based on celebrating the senses. Her joy in life was hard won through years of tough experiences, disappointments, and triumphs as a scientist and a human being. She is very down to earth, but her earthiness has a deep dignity.

We suspect this comes from Jane's awareness that she is a *creature*. Looking at photographs of her with her beloved animals, observing her delight in the natural world or the light in her eyes when she speaks with children and young people, it's apparent that she enjoys being a fellow creature.

Knowing you are a creature means knowing that you were *created*. Jane knows that she didn't spring forth spontaneously and she experiences herself in solidarity with all other mortal creatures. Every day is a gift and every tree and animal a brother or sister. This is the insight of St. Francis. Savoring the life of the senses means experiencing life as a gift in all its fragility. It means being open to a demanding solidarity with all creatures.

Alan has recently spent some time considering his dog, Sophie:

The other day I was watching Sophie busily being herself, chasing her tail and trying to herd us into the kitchen. I couldn't help thinking of a couple of lines from the eighteenth-century poet Christopher Smart: "For I will consider my Cat Jeoffrey. / For he is the servant of the Living God duly and daily serving him." I laughed when I thought of Sophie as a servant of the living God. But it got the wheels turning in my mind.

"For I will consider my Dog Sophie. For she is the servant of the Living God." When I repeated that phrase, something popped in my mind and I see myself in a deeper solidarity with the other animals than I did before. It also turned Sophie into a teacher for me. I

watch her more closely now—totally embodied, totally herself. I
wish I were more like her.

Being present to the sensuous is also a challenge to stretch our
imagination. The way we imagine things matters, because it will determine how we experience them. If we imagine that everyone we meet
is a rogue and out to cheat us, we experience the world differently
from someone who imagines that everyone is a potential ally or possible friend. If we imagine our dog or cat as "a servant of the living
God," we can experience our pet in a different way from someone who
sees it as just another household object.

We can well envy our fellow creatures their effortless ease in their
own bodies, or the keenness of their specialized senses, far surpassing
ours in some cases. We can learn about total engagement and true rest
by observing or living with them. But we can also rejoice in our
uniquely human ability to admire their physical splendor (and that of
our fellow humans). We can exercise our imagination to create art
with our hands and bodies, often interpreting or celebrating the forms
and movements of living creatures. And we can use our moral sense to
show solidarity with the rest of Creation, being in our own way "ser-
vants of the Living God."

Body Image and Exercise

Part of what we admire in other creatures is their physical aptitude,
often coming close to perfection in the prime of their relatively short
lives. Animals have good genetic reason to be so physically adept:
shaped either by the ruthless hand of natural selection or by rigorous
human breeding efforts. We humans are a much more variable species
in our degree of physical prowess and body type.

Until fairly recently, extraordinary human athleticism, beauty, grace,
or strength was celebrated but not obsessed over—as seems to be ever
more the case now. Blame for this obsession with body image has been
liberally spread around, and that's not our task here. But a few gentle
reminders might be in order. First, one needn't be a fabulous physical
specimen to enjoy a full and rewarding life of the senses. Second, we
believe there's a balance to be struck between commendable attempts

to stay healthy and fit well into later life, and the undignified lengths some go to in order to (essentially) hide from their mortality.

That said, our efforts to stretch and strengthen and tone our bodies can have a role in sharpening sensory capacities and enriching our life of the senses. Improved circulation can enhance smell, taste, and touch. A raised sense of physical well-being generally can help us feel more in tune with the world, more ready to notice and absorb details around us. John offers the example of his own walking practice as an easily accessible way into gratitude.

Walking Meditation

To me a walking meditation is a grand celebration of the senses, a joyous occasion, or it can be. I'm not sure when my walks on the Sausalito streets where I live turned the corner and became a celebration of gratitude. It was a big change but a gradual one, with no epiphany. It may have begun with the help of my wife, who is a very good observer of nature, especially birds. The Buddhist teachings of awareness, walking with the breath, may have helped too. Or it may be that spontaneous prayers simply took over the walk.

In my old way of walking, I was always in a hurry, head down, mind filled with worries, regrets, and tomorrow's challenges. From time to time I'd be aware of a beautiful view of San Francisco, but the exercise was the main purpose.

Now my walks are exercise not just for my legs and heart but for all my senses. My eyes are often drawn to certain plantings in a garden or a massive flow of cottony clouds. Sometimes aromas arrest my attention, shift the meditation. I use the walk to reflect on the blessings I possess: good health and family, work I enjoy, freedom of choice, talents I can grow. Occasionally gratitude comes in large gulps—seeing a newborn child, for example, or a friend recovering from a crushing illness. But the daily walk—stretching all the senses, putting things in perspective, reminding me of my world's wonders—guarantees at least small helpings of thankfulness, even on troubled days.

Body and Soul

> When you touch a body, you touch the whole person, the intellect,
> the spirit, and the emotions.
>
> —JANE HARRINGTON

François Rabelais, a brilliant scholar and physician of the early six-
teenth century, provoked scandal with his wildly sensual and scatolog-
ical tale *Pantagruel*. His adventures, punctuated with gross anecdotes,
featured the search for a great bottle full of good things, meals for
giants involving the slaughter of thousands of cattle, and a lot of scato-
logical references to bodily functions. In this work of vast imagination,
Rabelais attacked monks and theologians because they did not honor
the body and were frightened of the senses—and he got in a lot of
trouble for it.

Rabelais insisted that the basis of life is physical and good and
refuted with humor the terrible notion that the body is merely sinful.
He is said to have coined the maxim, "To laugh is natural to man." He
saw our physicality as the power that spurs us to achieve, the means
by which we express all that we are. To Rabelais, our indulgences with
food and sex look more comical than degrading. We should hold them
lightly and give more weight to deeper issues of malice and injustice in
evaluating human morals.

Indeed, it is only through our bodies that we can know the divine,
as all the great faiths have acknowledged at one time or another. The
theologians of Rabelais's time were fond of a code word for things of
the spirit needing to be enfleshed: *incarnation,* or enfleshment. In one
of the Jewish Kabbalist cults, a believer was instructed to imagine that
each of his limbs was an earthly shrine for the Divine Presence. This
was part of elaborate ritual efforts to end humanity's separation from
the Godhead.

To Christians, of course, Jesus was "spirit made flesh"—the ultimate sacrifice made by a loving incarnated God to save humankind
when all instruction and prophecy had failed. And Siddharta Gau-
tama, the Buddha, had to descend to the depths of physical degrada-
tion to eventually point the way to nirvana.

In pursuing any spiritual practice, it's important to keep in mind that we do not worship just with our minds. To follow certain mystical paths one must strive to transcend the body, but their teachings recognize this as a mighty struggle. Most religious traditions take care to involve the senses in the search for contact with the divine. We (according to our faiths) chant, sing, shout in witness, or ring temple bells; we breathe incense and burning herbs; we consume symbolic bread and wine, or mushrooms. We create soaring vaulted spaces that lead the eye to heaven, or golden, many-armed statues, or brushwork that induces contemplation. We shake and sway, prostrate ourselves to earth, and dance. The gifts of our senses are sacred.

Come Back to the Real

Living a truly embodied life isn't easy. One of the purposes of working at deep gratitude is to dislocate the structures imprisoning our lives so that we can see something new. Dislocation prepares us for revelation. Gratitude tells us that we can't stand on the sidelines. It calls us to be keenly present—to our particular body, our particular history, the place and time where we are living. Each of us is called to be available to life in an attitude of trust. Attending to the life of the senses helps us to be fully available.

Anne Tyler, in her novel *Dinner at the Homesick Restaurant,* tells the story of Pearl Tull, a woman abandoned by her husband to bring up three children, who is now old, blind, and dying. Every day her son Ezra reads to her a passage from her journal. It's frankly pretty boring—but one day, when she is close to death, Ezra reads:

> "Early this morning, I went out behind the house to weed. Was kneeling in the dirt by the stable with my pinafore a mess and the perspiration rolling down my back, wiped my face on my sleeve, reached for the trowel, and all at once thought, Why I believe that at just this moment I am absolutely happy."
>
> His mother stopped rocking and grew still.
>
> "The Bedloe girl's piano scales were floating out of her window," he read, "and a bottle fly was buzzing in the grass, and I saw that I was kneeling on such a beautiful green little planet. I don't care what else might come about, I have had this moment. It belongs to me."

It was the end of the entry. He fell silent.

"Thank you, Ezra," his mother said, "There's no need to read any more."

Pearl is given this moment through all her senses. She can smell the green world all around her. She hears the piano and the bottle fly. She feels her own sweat in the hot sun. She experiences deep gratitude, and it enables her to let go, to move on. She has understood that the world is a gift. Like freshly baked bread. The bread has risen! The oven is still hot! Can't you smell it? Come and get it!

Tune Your Senses

Each of our senses is a doorway to different experiences of gratitude and wholeness. As Pearl's example shows, life's transcendent moments come when all the senses are working together at full power. A well-tuned appreciation of sensory experience keeps us grounded in the here and now, and helps us knit past and present together.

As we briefly survey the gifts of the senses below, you'll find simple exercises and practices to try. The only thing hard about these exercises is that they require our taking time. Your aim in all of these practices is to increase awareness of sensory experience, which will help you become more frequently and gratefully aware of life as a gift for your savoring.

Gratitude Practice: In-sight

Ruler of the senses, sight is the path by which we access so much of life's richness. We depend on it to navigate the perils of existence, to learn the meaning of our immediate environment and the history of our species, to read each others' faces and body language. In combination with our interior vision, we use it to create and appreciate literary and visual forms of art.

The human eye alone is an astounding mechanism, far more subtle than any camera lens at discerning form and detail even in low

light, such as the melting of sunset into dusk. But the combined ability of eye and brain is truly among humankind's great wonders. As
researchers in artificial intelligence have discovered, a computer can
fairly easily be made to see but is nearly hopeless at interpreting what
it sees, less adept than any infant. So dependent are we on the accumulated experience of eye and brain working in tandem that when
confronted with a totally unfamiliar sight we may fail to "see" it at all—
like the natives of Tierra del Fuego, who, it is said, barely noticed
when Magellan reached their shores. The sight was so strange that
they couldn't decode the visual evidence.

What we believe to be true depends on the richness and power of
our imagination. How do we decode the evidence in front of our eyes?
The poet William Blake asked a man what he saw when he looks at the
sun. "I see a disk in the sky rather like a guinea," was the answer. Blake
was appalled. He saw no such mundane thing as a gold coin. He saw a
blazing sign of the Lord of Hosts! The world offers a million things a
day to see. But things truly reveal themselves only when outer and
inner vision work together.

To tune your appreciation of sight (and grow in "in-sight"), we'll
challenge you, first, to look more closely and consciously at familiar
things. Take a few moments to focus on a detail of your surroundings
with total attention and without judgment (ignore that the dining
room table needs dusting). Describe it as if you were painting a verbal
picture for someone who has never seen this object before. Notice the
assumptions and associations that find their way into your description.
You may find yourself using evidence of the other senses to help your
word painting (what is it like to touch?), and that's fine. What do you
discover about your perceptions of this thing? If you find something
that is especially pleasurable or rewarding to see deeply in this way,
you might make a regular meditation exercise with it, in the way that
Buddhists use mandalas or sand paintings.

Another exercise is to pause for contemplation when you see
something for the very first time. How many times in a given day does
this happen to you? (It can be useful to spend a whole day noting first-
time sights—not on a trip to a strange place but in your everyday life.)
What do you draw on from your experience and imagination to give
meaning to the new sight?

Gratitude Practice: Hear Sounds

The gifts of hearing can stir the heart like no other: a loved one's voice, a child's laugh, a hawk's cry or wolf's howl, an inspired piece of music. The survival value of sound also is deeply embedded in our bodies and collective consciousness: a cry of alarm, a warning siren, the growl of a beast ready to charge. Hearing may be the sense most assaulted by modern life, at least for those who live in urban areas, and we'd do well to strive for improved awareness of sounds that please and feed our spirits, as well as those with the opposite effect.

Here's a group exercise Alan once took part in to tune the perception of sound. You can adapt it for use on your own by assembling some familiar objects that can make noise, and randomly acting upon each to produce sound, preferably with your eyes closed.

Imagine a group of, say, fifteen people in a room. Each is asked to find something on their person with which to make a noise: a bunch of keys, a pen or pencil, a shoe, a piece of paper. The instructor tells them to close their eyes, and asks them to make their particular noise only when she touches them lightly on the shoulder, then to stop when she touches them a second time. She also asks them to notice the silence in the room before the noise begins. Slowly she goes around the room, touching a shoulder here and there, until the whole room is filled with the racket of jangling keys, pens hitting chairs, and shoes being bashed on the floor. As she circulates the second time, the noises trail off and there is silence once more—a deeper and more palpable silence than the first. The ear is more awake to sound and its absence.

Gratitude Practice: Smell and Taste Things

These senses are often the most direct gateway to memory, in part because they are linked with the power of food to evoke past experience—most famously with Proust and his madeleines! Alan reports that certain foods unfailingly take him back to a certain place and time:

One whiff of rosemary and I am cooking lamb for twenty in New York two decades ago. The smell of roasted peppers always reminds me of the friend who first taught me to roast them in the oven and then steam them in a paper bag before peeling. I can vividly recall our delight in each other's company as we covered the peeled peppers with garlic and olive oil.

When I visit England in summertime, I beg my relations to buy red and black currants and bake a pie. I am then transported back to my childhood and my mother's cooking—berries piled high, the pastry scored with a fork, and, oh, the smell! Other foods remind me of special rituals when my children were growing up. I cannot eat a pancake (or more accurately a crepe) without thinking of Saturday mornings. Saturday meant pancakes. And not the flapjack kind with blueberries and syrup, but thin English pancakes with sugar and lemon juice.

All of us can probably play this game with certain foods.

Here are a couple of things you can do to raise your conscious appreciation of tastes and smells. Try eating something much more slowly than you normally do, focusing on all aspects of the experience: odor, texture, degree of sweet or salt, sour or bitter. Wine tasters do this all the time, but anyone can hone their taste buds with a little focused effort. A teacher friend of Alan's gave each of his students a pitted black olive and asked them to eat it as slowly as possible. One of the students experienced a minor revelation. He thought he liked olives. He'd been used to thoughtlessly wolfing them down. It was only when he took the time really to taste them that he found them disgusting both in flavor and texture.

You may find that this exercise starts to affect the way you prepare food, or the foods you choose. Alan, who is on a strict vegetarian diet as part of a health study, discovered that his taste for seasonings changed:

As part of the study I have to drink 16 ounces of low-sodium tomato juice every day. At first the juice tasted revolting or, rather, it didn't taste of anything. So I added lots of Tabasco. After about a month on the diet I discovered I could taste things in a way that I couldn't before. Now the juice is full of flavor and doesn't need spicing up.

You might experiment with reactivating your taste buds. Try eating your favorite foods without smothering them with condiments. They may taste bland at first, but over time the flavors emerge in a fresh way. You still may want to add something, but it won't be as much.

Gratitude Practice: Feel Things

Think of all the things we handle every day—including each other. If we slow down enough to notice, countless things we do can be exercises in tactile awareness. Alan loves scratching and stroking his dog, "because she enjoys it and because of the different textures of her hair—soft and silky on her head and chest, coarse and rough on her back near her tail." One enjoyable way to heighten the sensation of touch is to get a ball of clay and mold it into a shape that's pleasing. Probably best of all is simply to notice how something feels when you touch it: the keys to your house, the clothes you put on, the warmth of a coffee mug, the textures and temperatures of the hands you shake in a given day.

Another experiment heightens awareness of touch while involving the other senses as well. Take a rough piece of wood—small enough to handle easily—and a sheet of sandpaper, and just smooth out the wood with the paper. It's a satisfying experience, as wordworkers can attest: the changing feel of the wood, the smell of the sawdust, the rhythmic sound of sanding, and the sight of the wood coming alive in a new way. You can almost taste the wood as it gives off the sawdust.

Let's end with a story. A friend of ours works downtown, heading the Human Resources Department in a big corporation. She's good at her job and her company has a lot of confidence in her. One day last fall, a fellow employee who was also a good friend of hers had a massive heart attack at work and died on the way to the hospital. He lived with his wife and three children (all under ten) in a great fixer-upper across town. Our friend, Sasha, was anxious that the widow not get the news from strangers, so it happened that she arrived at the house at the same time the police were knocking on the door.

The new widow received the news and froze. She couldn't move or speak. The kids were occupied with the television. Sasha didn't know what to do, so she went to the woman, put her arms around her, and just held her tightly. After while there was movement—a heaving of the shoulders—and Sasha led her to the sofa, where they held each other until the tears came. Sasha remained silent the whole time.

Later she said, "It was very strange. There were no words, but something held us together. Life was being shared through the sweat between pressed cheeks and the wetness of tears on clasped hands. I'll never forget it."

Our senses not only give us pleasure. They bring us meaning.

10

Sweet Rest

Clocks cannot tell our time of day
For what event to pray,
Because we have no time, because
We have no time until
We know what time we fill,
Why time is other than time was.
—W. H. AUDEN, "NO TIME"

Brenda never took time off. How could she? Her mother had diabetes and congestive heart failure; her father had begun a long, gradual decline into the fog of Alzheimer's disease. After an eight-hour day at her legal assistant job, Brenda began her second shift: taking care of her parents. She spent many weekends and evenings in pharmacies and hospital emergency rooms; every time the phone rang, she braced for bad news.

The bad news came much closer to home. While dusting the hard-to-reach top shelves of the kitchen, Brenda slipped off the kitchen ladder and broke her hip. Surgery repaired the break, but the rupture in her life proved harder to mend. Suddenly, Brenda had time on her hands. After years of nonstop activity, she hardly knew what to do with herself.

Some friends came to the rescue, inviting Brenda to recuperate for a month at their home on the coast just south of San Francisco. There was a deck with an ocean view, and on the deck was a hammock. She had to be helped into the hammock, but once she settled back, Brenda discovered just how tired—deep-down, bone-weary exhausted—she had been.

We visited her on a hot August afternoon and found her looking strangely serene. "I've never enjoyed such sweet rest," she said. "'Sweet'? What do you mean?" we asked. "It's a kind of rest new to me. Sure, I've felt great after a good night's sleep. But this is different. This rest goes much deeper than anything I've experienced before. It's not just rest for the body. It's rest for me. It's rest from me. To tell the truth, I was getting sick of my life, sick of myself. This rest is gentle. It's healing. It's fun. Yes, it's sweet."

Like Brenda, we all need to take a sabbatical from our selves now and then. We need to slip into that hammock on the deck and doze off. We need lazy summer afternoons, Sabbath time, catnaps. Saint Augustine described God as *semper agens, semper quietus*—always active, always at rest. We mortals need to follow a different rhythm: sometimes active, sometimes at rest.

Rest comes in different guises, each sweet in its way. And they don't always involve actual sleep. There's the gratifying contentment of finally getting horizontal after a long, hard day of work. (In Alan's family, the phrase for this kind of rest was always, "I think I'll take a long, soaky bath.") How about plopping into a deck chair with a cold beer or iced tea after a couple of hours mowing the lawn and tidying up the yard? Or the pleasant half-doze on a rainy weekend morning when nothing urgent is calling you?

The best thing about such experiences is that they are available to us every day. The trouble is we tend to fall into them by accident rather than to program them into our lives as a natural counterpart to activity. We forget to be grateful for the healing power of rest, and we neglect to make "sweet rest" part of our practice of gratitude. And the more tired we are, the less capable we are of being fully awake and present in our lives.

Oh, for a Good Night's Sleep!

How long—and how well—did you sleep last night? If you responded "eight hours" and "like a baby," you're in the minority. According to Dr. William C. Dement, founder and director of the Stanford University

Sleep Research Center, Americans on average sleep one and a half fewer hours each night than our great-grandparents did a century ago.

Our society rewards achievement, alertness, even restlessness, and regards sleep and rest as slacking off. We admire Thomas Edison—inventor of the incandescent light bulb, which allows us to extend our daytimes indefinitely—because he claimed to sleep only four hours a night. (In fact, he took frequent naps during the day.) Sleep, we think, is optional—a waste of time. We may deserve a luxury car or a spacious condo, as the advertisements tell us, but rest? The very notion seems foreign. Even our pursuit of leisure sounds like hard work. "I work hard and I party hard!" says one of our friends, speaking for many.

What we conveniently forget is that our biology hasn't caught up with the day-lengthening advances of the last century or so. "We have grown so accustomed to living year round in an artificial summer of light, with long days and short nights, that it is hard to imagine life before electric lights and modern work schedules," writes Dement. "But our bodies haven't forgotten." Over countless millennia, our bodies became tuned to circadian clocks: internal chronometers that respond to the daily sunrise and sunset and to the seasonal waxing and waning of daylight. Our "electric cave," as Dement poetically puts it, cannot completely counteract our genetic inheritance. When sunlight fades, our eyelids droop. It's time to rest.

Cycle of Dark, Cycle of Light

The poet David Whyte asks us to consider this common situation: The phone rings and a friend asks us to jump in the car and spend an evening on the town. Now imagine replying, "I'm sorry, but I just don't leave the house in the last half of the month when the moon is growing smaller. I go out only in the first part of the month when the moon is growing larger." Laughable? Perhaps. But listen:

> We think we exist only when our life looks like the first half of the cycle, when our "moon" is waxing, when our sense of ourselves is growing and getting larger. . . . If things are dying or falling away, we dismiss it, we refuse to see it as the second half of the very same

cycle and think there is something "wrong" with us. We think something terrible has happened to us and we need to do a whole list of things to put it right. Much of our stress and subsequent exhaustion at work comes from our wish to keep ourselves at full luminescence all month, even when our interior "moon" may be just a sliver in the sky, or about to fade from sight altogether. It takes tremendous energy to keep up a luminescent front when the interior surface is fading into darkness.

The truth is, half the time, we are faking it. We fail to discern the value of downtime in the cycle of our lives. We even undervalue our time to sleep and to dream. We despise slowing down. Some of us are driven by a work ethic that confuses sleep with sloth, rest with inefficiency. To slow down and be still . . . well, as the song lyric puts it, "I'll sleep when I'm dead."

Learn to Relax

Some of us need to be taught to take real rest. As part of the Dean Ornish Prostate Program, Alan spends an hour a day practicing yoga and deep relaxation. His wife joins him. "I never really knew what it was to relax and I needed both to be taught and to be given the incentive to allow my body to catch up with itself every day," he says. "'Sweet rest' is now part of my daily routine, and it's contributed incalculably to my overall well-being. I had always felt that I needed to be *doing* something even in my times off. I needed to be reprogrammed. I now feel grateful for being alive."

We may feel the need for more rest yet pass over many opportunities to enjoy it. John has taken Winston Churchill as his model in this respect. "Churchill was a brilliant napper," he notes. "He could work around the clock with short naps insinuated into his schedule. He even designed a jumpsuit to wear that eliminated the fussy problem of wrinkled clothes and changing into sleep attire."

Churchill was also, of course, a monumentally prolific writer and one of the great statesmen of the twentieth century. It's comforting to think that napping—sweet rest—helped him replenish his prodigious energies.

Sabbath Rest

The concept of Sabbath—one day out of seven devoted to rest—was one of the great philosophical breakthroughs of ancient times. Today, it is honored at best perfunctorily, with a brief visit to church or synagogue, or (more likely) an afternoon spent watching a football game. "Sabbath observance" evokes a decidedly archaic religious fanaticism and a long list of "thou-shalt-nots."

But let's take a closer look. The origins of the Sabbath are in the Biblical Creation story: God labored for six days and on the seventh he rested. According to Abraham Joshua Heschel, the great Jewish scholar and theologian, the Sabbath was the Jews' supreme gift to the world. What makes it special, he says, is that it represents more than mere rest—more than recovery from labor to prepare us for a new week's labors. Instead, the Sabbath is an end in itself—not a means of gaining strength for new efforts but rather "a day for the sake of life." It is "not an interlude but the climax of living." The Sabbath is not for the sake of the weekdays, writes Heschel; "the weekdays are for the sake of the Sabbath."

Imagine setting aside a whole twenty-four hours each week to celebrate rest, reflection, comfort, and pleasure (for the Sabbath is about physical as well as spiritual nourishment—sex on the Sabbath, to religious Jews, is a commandment)! What would it take for you to devote a day to serious rest, sweet rest? Or even a half day?

Be Empty and Full

The concept of Sabbath speaks to our need for time out. It also speaks of a kind of emptiness, and emptiness is something most of us dread. Yet there is a kind of emptiness that we desperately need. Emptiness in this positive sense is related to glory (which simply means "being fully alive.")

There's a Zen parable about a young man who sits down to tea with the Zen Master. The master poured tea into his guest's cup until the tea overflowed and spilled onto the table. "What are you doing?" cried the young man. The master responded: "You are like this cup. You're so full of yourself that nothing can get in."

The mystics thought of emptiness as a fruitful place—a kind of womb of new possibilities. The "existential" self fills up over a lifetime "with attachment and worry and noise," according to the theologian Paul Tillich. By contrast, the emptied "essential self" is "simpler and more peaceful"—a vessel of peace. The metaphysical term is *kenosis*—literally, emptying out, purging. True glory—which means "being fully alive and aware," requires the kind of self-emptiness that comes only with rest.

Emptiness requires practice. Meditation is one of the many disciplines that help us come to a restful yet life-bearing place of emptiness. Sit still and concentrate on your breathing for five minutes. Your mind will wander. Simply and gently bring it back to your breathing. It takes practice but its rewards are great. Among those rewards is a deep gratitude for being alive and being aware.

Wait in the Moment

Sweet rest is not a matter of zonking out. It is not mere passivity but a kind of passionate waiting in the moment. There's a wise piece of advice from the Jewish tradition: "The key to everything is the way you start." We are beings who have expectations and from whom something is expected. A genuinely human being is one of whom demands can be made, who has the capacity to respond to what is required. The central problem is not: What is being? But rather: What is being asked of me?

What is demanded of us? Perhaps the thing to "do" after times of sweet rest is deceptively simple. Make that phone call. Write that letter. Don't say, "I will never touch another cigarette!" Better to take it one day at a time.

Sweet rest comes from an appropriate love of self. And proper love of self springs from the practice of gratitude. It involves taking responsibility for your future and trusting it.

Gratitude Is Attitude

Imagine a woman ironing. She may be working for a laundry at minimum wage to make ends meet. She may be ironing a dress for a night on the town or ironing her lover's shirt out of love. Perhaps it's simply what she does on every Monday, week after week. The point is that it's all *work*. How it is conceived will depend on circumstances and attitude. We have choices, more than we realize, with regard to attitude. Resignation or expectation? A smile or a scowl? Life is a strange mixture of choice and necessity. There's not much we can do about necessity but there's a lot we can do about choice. Gratitude is attitude.

Sweet rest does not remove the need for work; it is work's complement. Noel Coward, the playwright, is supposed to have said, "Work is much more fun than fun." When we understand *that*, "sweet rest" comes naturally to us because it is in the context of a job well done.

Gratitude Practice: Floor Relaxation

This is a simple practice that Alan learned from the cancer study program. It's appealing in its simplicity and its gentle effectiveness.

Pick your favorite piece of music—one that is quiet and relaxing—and lie on the carpet, the softer the better. You might want to have a light blanket over you. Now tense your right leg, hold it up an inch from the floor and let it drop. Do the same with the left leg.

Next, tense your arms and splay your fingers. Make gentle fists and raise them an inch or two and let them drop.

Repeat this tensing and letting go with other parts of your body: the buttocks, the shoulders, the head. You might end by tensing all the muscles of the face and then relaxing them. Then go over your body with your mind, gently telling each part to relax. Finally, allow the body to bring you to the edge of sleep as you enjoy the music. When the music comes to an end, come out of your practice slowly. Enjoy.

Gratitude Practice: Traveling Rest

John likes to practice this restful exercise when traveling, especially on long flights. Be dressed in very comfortable clothing. Remove your shoes. Put in earplugs or wear a headset with no sound coming in. Wear an eyeshade. Now meditate on what you have to be grateful for (this helps drive away the worry lists and anxieties that travel can bring). Pay attention to your breathing. Measure it carefully in the beginning and then stop worrying about it.

Set a mental alarm clock. It is amazing how well the mind reacts to autosuggestion. Science tells us that about 20 minutes is the right time for the most restorative nap. They say Winston Churchill's naps were about that long.

Sweet rest is lovely to grab while in a taxi, on a bus, on a plane, or at your desk. But sweet rest at 30,000 feet is especially gratifying since you really are free to use your time as you like.

Gratitude Practice: Take Time for Meditation

It is said that meditation is the art of doing one thing at a time. Simple? No! Try sitting in a comfortable position (not so comfortable that you'll fall asleep) and close your eyes and concentrate on your breathing. Just notice it and when your mind wanders don't berate yourself but simply refocus on your breathing. Do this for five minutes. Notice how you feel and where your mind is after this. There are other things you can do too, like concentrating on an object or on a word. The point is to allow the mind to rest in another place.

Alan has the following quotation from the poet W. B. Yeats framed in his study: "We can make our minds so like still water that beings gather about us that they may see, it may be, their own images, and so live for a moment with a clearer, perhaps even with a fiercer life because of our quiet."

Our taking time for ourselves is not a selfish act. It rebuilds the world.

PART III

Autumn

The Grateful Self

As our gratitude practice ripens into its autumn, we can begin to harvest the fruit of self-understanding and maturity. Giving thanks becomes an expression, even an imperative, of personal integrity or wholeness. From a grateful heart, truth telling and trust follow.

A banker we know named Melissa has been through a decade-long process of "reorienting" her identity. She's had to confront and thank a lot of dragons along the way. The first woman to rise to a high level in financial services at her big West Coast bank, Melissa was breaking glass ceilings every couple of years. Both consciously and not, she had to create a persona that could withstand the impact.

"I lowered my speaking voice to a growl after a client told me I sounded like a little girl on the phone." More seriously (and less consciously), she made herself physically rigid and emotionally manipulative. "I knew exactly how to make people feel bad," she says, "and I would use it when I needed to." She also had a powerful model in her own boss, a woman she describes as "a dark mirror for me."

At a meeting one day, she noticed that her left foot was swollen to twice its normal size. Doctors could find no good explanation; she even consulted an oncologist, who said, "You're too healthy to have cancer— but something's wrong here." Symptoms would mysteriously come and go, but her behavior didn't change. Until one morning, rushing from the subway, she took a hard fall and literally smashed her face in.

"That got my attention," Melissa says. Soon afterwards, she left the bank and her seventeen-year investment there. With a good package, she didn't need to work for a while, so she freelanced a bit, investigated bodywork, and indulged in voice lessons—reviving a childhood dream of becoming an opera singer. "That wasn't meant to be," she laughs, "but I discovered that my body was so frozen I couldn't sing higher than a few tones above middle C. Now I'm a soprano!"

Among the dragons Melissa faced in that time was the illness and death of her beloved younger brother from AIDS and the family conflict this engendered. She was in denial about how bad things were until her husband gently suggested that, since they were moving anyway, they find a place near Philip. She mourned her brother deeply and felt he had died in bitterness, until much later—at a memorial service for a man she hardly knew—she heard a voice telling her, "Don't worry; we've got him."

"And I feel 'held' now too," she says. "By my family, my church community, by myself. I've learned to care for myself." And this allows her to care for others. A bank where she freelanced offered a full-time position, and while she has a lot of responsibility, she feels that, "in a sense, I've retired." She often finds herself acting as a mediator. "People there ask me why I don't get upset when things get crazy. I guess the simple answer is that I know the 'me' who works there is just part of the whole 'me.'"

Melissa was proud of her rapid rise at the large bank, but ultimately more grateful for the experiences that prompted her to leave. At her new post she appreciates the chance to be mentor, as well as a less-pressured schedule that allows her time to travel—with her husband and parents she took an opera tour of Italy last year—and pursue new learning in music and spirituality. "I'm grateful most of all for being able to see myself as a work in progress!" she says, a true comment on autumnal ripening.

11

Going for Authentic Life

If we live long enough and deep enough and authentically enough,
gratitude becomes a way of life.

— MARK NEPO

The fruits of the harvest are gathered and stored. The trees shed
their leaves and reveal their true forms. The days grow shorter and
darker, reminding us of how brief our time on earth really is. It's
autumn: a season for reflecting on what it means to be truly alive, and
for giving thanks for the gifts an authentic life bestows.

It's no coincidence that *autumn* and *authenticity* are linguistic
cousins. Both share the Latin root *aut-*, meaning "to increase or grow."
Autumn brings the harvest bounty: the earth's increase. Authenticity
brings the reward of increased self-knowledge and awareness, of a life
augmented (another word cousin!) through integrity. As autumn represents the ripening of the crops, so authenticity represents the coming
into maturity of our characters. The link is gratitude, which allows us
to ground ourselves in humility and recognize our authentic nature.
When we live gratefully, we become more truly ourselves.

What Does Authenticity Look Like?

Authentic literally means "by one's own hand." An authentic document
isn't copied; it's created by an original maker—an *author,* a word that
shares that same *aut-* root.

When we live authentically, we are the authors of our own lives. We are in touch with everything that makes us unique: our genetic history, our cultural heritage, the sum of our experiences. And because we're grateful for these gifts, we avoid the traps of pretension and pomposity.

It's often difficult to identify the face of authenticity: there are so many expert copies! By the time we've entered school, most of us have acquired the ability to become chameleons, adopting a variety of psychic masks and costumes that we wear for different audiences. We can be charming pleasers or foot-stamping tantrum throwers as the occasion or mood warrants. As we grow up, the masks and costumes become second nature. We do things because we've always done them, respond in automatic patterns to the demands of our lives.

Yet if we're at all reflective, we recognize that these habits aren't "the real us." We feel dissatisfied because we're living inauthentically.

Some self-help guides advocate "just being true to yourself" as the antidote to this dissatisfaction. Too often, that translates in practice into, "I must follow my impulses regardless of the consequences for others." Selfishness may be the authentic nature of a newborn infant, but it's not the hallmark of a mature, aware adult. It's our responsibility to temper our authenticity with the moderating influences of gratitude and humility.

This is especially important for people in leadership positions to keep in mind. Success not balanced with gratitude can starve the soul and feed hubris, creating damaging distance between leaders and those they lead. Authentic leaders are truth tellers, especially about themselves, never allowing the role they play to define them. And they stay in touch with all that went into making them—the gifts of family, teachers, friends, and mentors—even when given enormous power. Expressing gratitude builds teamwork and anchors the leader to his or her foundation values. Leaders who cultivate a grateful spirit will be vital, durable, and capable of inspiring others.

Acting an Authentic Role

As a priest, Alan dresses up all the time—on a daily basis in a collar and black shirt, on festive occasions in gorgeous vestments. He sees himself as an actor in a very important play that touches the lives of countless people. But his authentic self is not dependent on dressing up.

No one can survive without wearing a costume. We all have to dress up in order to function in the world. Just as we sometimes pretend to be fearless to survive a challenge, we begin our authentic life with acting "as if" honesty and authenticity truly mattered.

Consider the lives and actions of the rescue workers who rushed to Ground Zero after the September 11 attacks. These firefighters, paramedics, and police officers certainly felt fear, but acted *as if* fear didn't matter. Their authentic selves prompted them to act selflessly and indeed courageously in the face of unthinkable horror. And they taught us one of the most significant lessons in gratitude we can ever hope to learn.

Distorted Images

In Hans Christian Andersen's classic fairy tale *The Snow Queen,* a demon invents a cruel mirror "which had the power of making everything good or beautiful that was reflected in it almost shrink to nothing, while everything that was worthless and bad looked increased in size and worse than ever." The mirror is carried up to heaven, but it falls to earth, shattering into millions of pieces. Some of the pieces land in people's eyes, causing them to see only the worst aspects of life. Other fragments strike people in the heart, "and this was very terrible, for their hearts became cold like a lump of ice."

Think of the distorting mirrors in our own lives, which make life ugly, distort our self-image, and harden our hearts against gratitude. We may suffer from the distortion of hubris or the distortion of entitlement. We may denigrate ourselves to the point where we see only a small, insignificant reflection. We may be incapable of seeing just how much we have to be grateful for. We need a new mirror, one made of trust and gratitude.

The truth is that looking at the world gratefully is more accurate than looking at it resentfully. The world is transformed into the lens through which we look at it. If you expect everyone in the room to act like an idiot, then it's likely to happen. If you expect to learn new things and find their company interesting and delightful, you probably will. Gratitude is related to authenticity because seeing the world as a gift that elicits our gratitude is a clearer and truer way of moving through life.

Discover Your Inner Equinox

We grow in maturity and authenticity when we find a proper balance between prudence and risk, between action and restraint, between words and silence. Autumn is a perfect metaphor for this balance. Fall comes between the fullness of summer and the barrenness of winter. The autumnal equinox—the beginning of autumn—is the day when the periods of light and dark are exactly equal.

In the Jewish calendar, the holiest days of the year fall around the autumnal equinox. These are the days, balanced between light and dark, when life itself is said to hang in the balance—when our naked, authentic souls are judged by God. Between Rosh Hashanah, the New Year, and Yom Kippur, the Day of Atonement, are the ten Days of Awe, when humans are obliged to seek forgiveness from people they've wronged during the previous twelve months. Then, on Yom Kippur, one stands before God and asks for forgiveness for transgressions against Him. The answer to that request is inscription in the book of life . . . or in its counterpart.

As somber as this occasion is, it's followed just five days later by Sukkot—the harvest-thanksgiving holiday. (In fact, Sukkot was the model for the Old Testament–reading American Pilgrims' first Thanksgiving.) Gratitude for the gifts of the earth—and for surviving another year—overflows on Sukkot.

Soon afterward is the holiday of Simchat Torah, which rejoices in the giving of the Torah, the five books of Moses. This final autumn festival gives voice to gratitude for the laws that govern human conduct.

Solemnity balanced by festivity, authenticity matched by gratitude: It's a balance we all must strive for. When there is no place in our
value structures for gratitude to take hold, we can become lost in false
self-definitions. To find the balance in your own life, ask yourself:
What am I grateful for throughout the year? What am I grateful for
right now? How does gratitude make me a more integrated and
authentic person?

Authentic Maturity

Alan used to dream that his mother would tell him the great family
secret when he reached the age of eighteen. "Who am I really, Mom?"
he'd ask. And she would respond, "You're really the bastard son of a
Russian prince with whom I had a brief affair when he was making
ends meet as a London taxi driver." When he grew up, Alan had to
accept that his real father was a bricklayer (and a good one at that!).
But the childhood fantasy was important to him because it nurtured
his belief that a human being was full of unrealized possibilities.

Flights of fancy are very important at certain stages in our lives—
for example, when only a cunning strategy will help you stay alive and
be true to yourself. At what point was it prudent and at what point was
it cowardly to give the Nazi salute in Germany during the Second
World War? At what point do you comply? At what point do you
protest?

In everyday life, though, we must learn to be grounded in reality.
The authentic life has been refined in the fires of experience and
comes out on the other side being able to trust the world as it is.

That trust may be hard won, because it involves acknowledging
that some things in life can't be fixed. We can't change our genetic
makeup, or the people to whom we're bound in family ties. We can't
change our cultural heritage, although we can learn about other cultures. We can't fix time—it travels in only one direction. Love can't be
demanded or bought. And death remains the great unfixable. Think of
what we do to avoid our mortality!

So much inauthentic living comes from our trying to ignore time, to cheat death, and to buy love. These strategies lead to resentment and bitterness. The strategy of grateful living allows us to accept the great unfixables as the container of our full and joyful life.

We all know people who define themselves by their age. One of John's former clients was a middle-aged businessman who sought to go live by engaging in extreme sports, just as he had seen younger men do. Such behavior is common enough for C. G. Jung, the Swiss psychoanalyst, to have given it a name: *puer aeternus,* eternal youth. We can be inauthentic by refusing to grow up.

We also know people who go in the opposite direction and define themselves as prematurely old. We watch young people pull back from life, afraid, hunched, with boundaries tightly drawn. They are unwilling to risk or learn.

Imagine yourself at 70, 80, or 90. Your youth is dead. And you have a choice: You can refuse to let go of your lost youth. If you do that you will be blocking transformation and you will be unhappy, fearful, and frustrated because you have forgotten how to be grateful.

Or you can choose to let go of the past and be grateful for the present. As we let go of the things that have died on us, new life emerges in the grateful heart. What a gift to be able to say, "It was good to be 20, 30, 40, 50, 60—it's even better to be 70!"

Gratitude Transforms Us

Gratitude can transform even the harshest of "true" stories into authentic opportunities for wonder and growth.

Viktor Frankl, who was an inmate in Auschwitz during World War II, tells of a transforming moment as he was stumbling to work in the icy wind before dawn, one of the detachment of slaves driven by guards using rifle butts. Suddenly his wife entered his mind.

> Real or not, her look was then more luminous than the sun which was beginning to rise. A thought transfixed me: for the first time in my life I saw the truth as it is set into song by so many poets, proclaimed as the final wisdom by so many thinkers; that love is the ultimate and the highest goal to which man can aspire. I grasped the meaning of the greatest secret that human poetry and human

thought and belief have to impart: the salvation of man is through love and in love. I understood how a man who has nothing left in the world may still know bliss. . . . In utter desolation, when man cannot express himself in positive action, when his only achievement may consist in enduring his sufferings in the right way, man can achieve fulfillment. For the first time in my life I was able to understand the meaning of the words, "The angels are lost in perpetual contemplation of an infinite glory."

How is it that a man like Viktor Frankl experiences gratitude in the most degrading of circumstances, while others more fortunate move blindly through life, ungrateful for the world's wonders? We can only conclude that the capacity for gratitude is innate. It lies within each of us, waiting only for acknowledgement to grant us its blessings.

Bedrock and Sand

In one of the Gospels, Jesus tells a parable of two men who built houses—one on bedrock, the other on sand—and the consequences. A self-definition built on bedrock can withstand the howling storms and violent shakes of life, whereas a self-definition anchored in sand will not survive. Here are some examples:

Sand
- Standing on achievements. Saying, "I did that!"
- Using money or fame to keep score.
- Undervaluing the offerings of others who serve you.
- Leveling those who disappoint you and whinging when the fates frown.
- Feeling entitled.
- Harboring feelings of resentment, jealousy, outrage when others succeed.

Bedrock
- Recognizing that most of the difficult bits of life (the unfixables) are simply outside the reach of our will. We cannot will our children's success or our mate's love. We cannot will good health.

The sooner we place gratitude up front in our life view the less we will believe in our willful power.

- Laughing, whistling, and singing because life is good and joy must be expressed.
- Appreciating fully and consistently the smallest gift of courtesy bestowed by unlikely givers: the waitress who catches our sadness and smiles a portion of it away; the unknown and unseen driver who gives us room to enter the long traffic line.
- Knowing that the thinnest of edges separates robust health and debilitating disease and appreciating the everyday gift of well being.
- Finding great joy in the faces of happy children, a small boost from a friend, a quiet moment in a hectic day.
- Taking nothing for granted and expecting nothing in return for gifts and kindnesses offered except the feelings that go with giving freely.

Gratitude Practice: Discerning Authenticity

We all learn coping strategies as children that, as they solidify into habit, can prevent us from living authentically. Some common strategies are:

- Anger and hostility—a tendency to lash out
- Shutting down emotionally
- Identifying so strongly with other people that you forget your own identity
- Finding fault
- Avoiding conflict

What is your coping strategy? How does it prevent you from living authentically and expressing gratitude?

Think of two or three important turning points in your life, when you experienced what Charles Handy calls "discontinuous learning"— times when you had nothing to fall back on. Examples might include falling deeply in love, the sudden death of a loved one, a loss of financial security, a natural disaster. How did these events force you to learn and mature?

When do you feel most authentic? When you're alone? With other people? At work? In nature? Write a paragraph, or draw a picture, expressing your gratitude for a particular kind of authenticity.

What are you grateful for in autumn? Be as specific and honest as possible: "The red leaves on the Japanese maple tree." "My kids' returning to school—the house is quiet again!" "Knowing that Thanksgiving is just around the corner." Make your own list and come back to it each autumn.

12

Your Sustaining Narrative

Gratitude makes sense of our past, brings peace for today, and creates a vision for tomorrow.

— MELODY BEATTIE

"Once upon a time . . ."

Reading those words, did you automatically settle back and relax in pleasurable expectation? The classic beginning to countless stories has that effect on us: it's as though our brains were hardwired to receive stories—and to invent them.

According to the Canadian journalist and critic Robert Fulford, "Stories are the building blocks of human thought; they are the way the brain organizes itself." The Danish writer Isak Dinesen put it even more directly: "To be a person is to have a story to tell."

Since the days of our cave-dwelling ancestors, humans have entertained one another with tales that recapitulate ("What a great hunt we had!"), explain (". . . and that's why thunder happens"), and speculate ("After we die, we go to a beautiful country where we want for nothing"). Today, our movies and novels fulfill the same purpose as the stories Chaucer's pilgrims or Bocaccio's stranded travelers told each evening: They instruct us, distract us, and connect us in the bonds of a shared culture.

The stories we inherit are the foundations of our selves; the more stories we know, the more choices we have for modeling our behavior and our relationships. The stories we *create* are no less significant: They can limit us to tortured plot lines and unhappy endings, or they can show us how to be grateful three-dimensional actors in our life's narrative. To live authentically and move deeper into the practice of gratitude, we must find sustaining narratives and learn how to live them.

The Damaging Story

The terrorists of September 11 looked for a story that would justify their terrible acts. "Stand fast. . . . The time of fun and waste has gone. The time of judgment has arrived." These words—the thesis of the terrorists' narrative—were an exhortation in some instructions found in their luggage.

The terrorists had a story, all right—an apocalyptic, dogmatic story that allowed no opposition. In its way, this story is as damaging as no story at all. The denouements, as we've seen, are tragically similar—horrifyingly violent.

Apocalyptic narratives are hardly new, although the means to realize them are distinctly modern. In anxious times, how we choose to interpret experience becomes especially crucial, because choosing "doom and gloom" as a way of seeing the world becomes a self-fulfilling prophecy. If I see the world as a hopeful place, I will behave accordingly. The stories we choose to tell will help us interpret our experience.

In an essay written shortly after September 11, the novelist Don DeLillo writes, "Terror's response is a narrative that has been developing over years, only now becoming inescapable." Do we have an alternative story that takes into account the narrative of terrorism?

The Life-Saving Story

Compare the previous story to that of Terry Waite. Waite, the special envoy of the Archbishop of Canterbury, was held hostage in Beirut for 1,763 days—nearly five years—between 1987 and 1991. He spent much of that time in solitary confinement. Among his many privations was the absence of pencils and paper. Yet he refused to sink into despair. Using the only tools available to him—memory and imagination—Waite told himself his life story. On the bleakest days, the story sustained him. In his memoir, *Taken on Trust,* he writes, "I always managed to return to my story and thus was enabled to preserve my sanity and identity."

Terry Waite's story is both personal and universal. He was able to place his personal fears and circumstances in the context of a larger story, which carried him through an unimaginable trial. He survived because he believed not only that his life told a meaningful story but that the universe told one as well.

The Narrative that Sustains

What makes a sustaining narrative? What nourishes us as we navigate the ups and downs of life? Most important, how do we shape a story that encourages gratitude rather than rage, spite, or self-pity?

Here are some of the elements that help us build our story. None is sufficient on its own—terrorists believe they are part of something larger than themselves, but that "something" lacks the all-important generous vision and potential for revision. How many of these elements exist in your own narrative?

- The concept that we are part of something bigger than ourselves. The stories we inherit from grandparents and great-grandparents, directly or indirectly, help us understand our family history. Stories about the history of our neighborhood, city, and country help us feel like participants in a community with a shared purpose. Creation stories and other religious narratives help us find ourselves in the universe.
- The message that life is a gift. We need stories that encourage our sense of wonder at life's blessings and nourish our sense of gratitude.
- The promise of hope. Our story must be contained by some spiritual vision: we need to know not only what is but also what might be.
- A generous vision. Our story must posit being alive and aware as a privilege and an adventure.

- The possibility of revision. We need to know that we can rewrite our story as our life unfolds, because we must change our stories in order to grow.

Our capacity for gratitude is directly related to the kind of story we live. Our capacity for gratitude will determine whether we see life as a banquet to which everyone is invited or a fortress from which most people must be excluded.

Learn Who You Are

The first story we all must learn is the one about our own identity. Often, our stories about who we are are dictated by our parents and teachers; too often they go unquestioned and unexamined. But that doesn't mean we lack the power to alter them.

Suzanne was told as a child that she couldn't carry a tune; she quickly learned to keep her mouth closed when classmates sang Christmas carols or "The Star-Spangled Banner." Then she married a musician.

> Mike refused to believe I couldn't sing—he was always encouraging me to try. After we had a child I realized I wanted more than anything to sing "Happy Birthday" to our son. Mike brought me into his recording studio and set everything up. Somehow, being surrounded by all that professional equipment made me feel like someone else—someone who could sing! Or at least, someone who didn't care. We did take after take of me singing, with Mike adding musical backgrounds and sound effects until I liked the results. I was thrilled—I felt like Madonna! Now I sing all the time—mostly at home, it's true, but without fear or shame. I've become a person with a voice of my own.

When Alan was a child, he was told "people like us" need to know their place and "the likes of us" do not play tennis or go skiing. Because his parents felt overshadowed by their poor economic circumstances, they told a story about limits and fatalism. Another set of parents, in similar circumstances, might have told a very different story about seeing beyond the immediate horizon. Alan was able to rewrite the story he inherited and find a way out of the circumscribed world it portrayed.

We know people who grew up with the opposite story: a story about entitlement. They grow up arrogant and demanding, incapable of perceiving their own failings—incapable of understanding why they should experience gratitude.

We have the power to rewrite our "Who am I?" story from a generous, grateful perspective. If astonishment is the beginning of a spiritually mature take on life, choosing a generous view of the world and living gratefully are the seeds of the primary virtues of faith, hope, and love.

Gratitude Practice: Who Am I?

Think of how you tell your "Who am I?" story to a new coworker, friend, or lover. Do you always cast yourself in the role of a victim? A victor? Listen to the language you use to talk about your personality and your accomplishments. How would you like to change the structure of your narrative? Choose one element to change and write a brief "script" for your next telling. Is your new story convincing? Does it make sense? Does it honor your roots?

Who's the Victim in Your Story?

All stories have stock characters—the prince and princess, the villain, the cheeky maid or manservant, the garrulous old fool. Our personal story is no exception. We play various roles as the story of our life unfolds. One of the most popular—and damaging—is that of victim. Seeing ourselves as victims with no responsibility is one of the surest ways to prevent our becoming fully alive.

To be sure, playing the role of victim enables us to marshal our resentments, disappointments, and fears and forge them into a political and personal platform. The displaced and self-pitying self is the center of the narrative.

But the larger story tells us that each of us is part of a great *We*—the great human family—and thus linked with the lives of others. When we deny that life is that which we share with others, three things happen. We become

- Lonely, callous, and distrustful
- Seduced by the illusion of self-sufficiency
- Full of anxiety

How is shared purpose articulated? It once was conveyed in the stories we told around the campfire, in legends and tales kept alive by the elderly, and in the fairy tales and the fables told to children. A shared purpose with any vitality requires a sense of tradition, an historical imagination, and the cultivation of memory. These are the means by which time is redeemed and we begin again.

Live Generously

For generations, people have come to the United States in search of a new story, and many have found one. In its most elevated version, the story is about freedom; at its worst it's about power, greed, and wealth. Whichever version we tell, it is a sustaining story and has given millions a new sense of identity.

When Alan was sworn in as a new citizen in 1975, the Lower Manhattan courthouse was packed with representatives of what looked like every country in the world. The judge who swore them in told them the United States was an experiment in freedom and that citizenship had serious obligations. One of them was to live generously and gratefully so that others, including future generations, could enjoy the freedoms we take for granted.

That's the positive side of the American story. Here's the other.

Fred Korematsu grew up an American citizen in Oakland, California. But one Saturday afternoon in 1942, he was arrested and interned. His crime: being of Japanese ancestry. Being an American had been the dominant motif of Fred's personal story up until that moment. But his story conflicted with the national story, which labeled him a public enemy—and the bigger story won.

The Japanese-American experience leapt to mind in the wake of the terrorist attacks, when many Muslim Americans feared they were the objects of unfounded suspicion. Now more than ever, it's imperative that we consider our stories about the world in the light of generosity and inclusion—through the practice of gratitude for our shared humanity.

Gratitude helps us confront the cruelty and repression in communities that tell only one story in only one way (in families, churches, synagogues, temples, and cells). Some of the narratives of the past were horrendous—stories about race and class. We know from history what happens to people who won't be part of (or are assigned the role of outcast in) the story told by a Hitler, a Stalin, or an Idi Amin. Their fate echoes the ironic motto of the Jacobins, the advance guard of the French Revolution: "Be my brother or I will kill you!"

It's Never Too Late to Revise

Our personal stories have beginnings and middles, and will surely have endings as well. But because we can't know the endings, we must be open to revising our stories throughout our lives.

In doing so, we must be careful to revise in the light of honest self-appraisal and a grateful spirit rather than to cover up misdeeds or rationalize bad behavior. It's easy to create villains on whom we pin the blame for our suffering. It's harder to become the heroes we want to be.

We need to be conscientious editors, jettisoning the parts of our story than no longer further its development, adding elements that create a more unified and meaningful narrative—one that sustains us through the challenges of work and family life, one that gives us hope and strength.

Gratitude Practice: Examine Your Story

What story have you been telling yourself about yourself? Write it down. Where does it come from? Who is telling it? Where does it need correcting, trashing? If you can, show it to a trusted friend and then rewrite your story in the light of gratitude. To whom do you owe your skills, your gifts, all the things you like best about yourself? Say thanks!

Who are the villains in your life narrative? What would it take to rewrite their characters—to change them into more ambivalent or even positive figures? Try looking at them through the lens of gratitude: What did you learn from your negative experiences with these "villains"? Are you able to feel grateful for what you learned?

What is your Creation story? Every culture has a predominant Creation myth. What's yours? How does it inform your beliefs about human nature, the past, the present, and the future?

Try on a few roles. Find out if there's an improvisational acting group in your community. Join! It will provide a safe place for you to try on various roles and allow a new story to find itself.

13

Feeding Your Mind

A hundred times a day I remind myself that my inner and outer life depends on the labors of [others], living and dead, and that I must exert myself in order to give in the measure as I have received and am still receiving.

—ALBERT EINSTEIN

For many of us, autumn heralds a return to seriousness. Summer vacation and its outdoor pleasures are over, and willingly or not we go back to the classroom and the office. Our brains, which may have been on a "diet" all summer while we watched baseball games, tramped through the woods, or lazed on the beach, are now hungry for sustenance. It's time to stock our intellectual larder and give our minds the feast they deserve.

Cultivating an active intellect may seem to be a rather old-fashioned idea, not to mention a lot of work. Nowadays, we read for instant information or escapist entertainment; our computers handle our calculations; our television sets provide balm rather than stimulation on a chilly autumn evening. Besides, the very idea of *mind* strikes our modern ear as the cold antithesis of *heart:* arid, unfeeling, and mechanical.

But the mind is far from devoid of feeling and appetite, and the work of nurturing it can be as effortless and as natural as, well, eating. Just consider some of the language we use to talk about our intellectual lives. We *devour* a great novel. We *digest* a difficult concept. We say a provocative idea is *food for thought*. Face it, our brains are hungry! To stay aware and truly alive, they must be well nourished.

The Pleasures of Thought

When was the last time you felt grateful for your mind's abilities? Most of us take our intellect, with all its limitations and gifts, for granted. To appreciate how deeply satisfying our mental life can be, we may have to reach back to a childhood memory—of the first time we grasped the concept of long division, or memorized a part in a play, or learned the rules of chess.

Alan remembers the joy on his young daughter's face when, after what seemed like many hours of working on her first big jigsaw puzzle, she triumphantly put in the last piece and the picture was complete. We see the same expression on the faces of our scientist friends when a new insight reveals itself to them. They haven't lost that "childlike" love of a mental workout. Best of all, they are just as exhilarated and grateful when they are proved wrong—when a hypothesis has been tested and found inadequate. It's all part of the endless process of learning.

You don't have to have a Ph.D. to share in that pleasure. Think of our love of word play in jokes, or our delight in recognizing a tune on the radio . . . and then remembering the lyrics. How about working on a particularly difficult sentence in a book or a poem and suddenly it clicks? "Aha!" we say, "So that's what it means!" We're grateful for the gift of comprehension.

The Passionate Mind

Over the past hundred years we have lost the original connection of mind to spirit. Psychiatry bears some of the blame: When Freud's English translator wanted an equivalent for Freud's *seelisch* (from the German for "soul") he chose *mental;* this made Freud sound "scientific" but lost much of the original word's richness, its blend of intellect and feeling. In fact, it got us into trouble by pushing psychology and psychiatry in a mechanistic, "fix-it" direction, often doing a dis-service to those they were trying to help.

An earlier age didn't make this mistake. The thirteenth-century poet Dante wrote in *The Inferno* of the damned who had lost "the good of intellect." By "intellect" he meant the combination of intelligence and intuition, the ability to discern and discriminate. The doors of Hell were open for those who deliberately refused to see how things were properly *related* one to another. By contrast, Dante imagined Heaven to be filled with the joyful perception of all things related in unimaginable diversity.

To the ancients, the intellectual life wasn't about the mere accumulation of facts; it was an open system. Questions led to answers, and also to deeper and more penetrating questions. The Socratic method of teaching never answers a student's question directly. The teacher counters the inquiry with another question. Why? Because answering a question directly merely reinforces the student at the level at which the question was asked. A new question allows new levels of understanding to be opened and explored.

One of the tests of a first-rate intelligence is its ability to function—indeed, to enjoy the tension—while balancing two opposing ideas. Hard thinking is a spiritual task because, "Ideas we have, *and do not know we have,* have us," as the aphorism goes.

When we become possessed and obsessed by an idea, we become fanatical. We lose a sense of proportion. We fail to value things in the right order. We lose touch with love. We become enslaved by fixations and obsessions. No wonder that when we feel the liberating power of a free intellect we experience joy, relief, and gratitude. Thank you!

Learn Something!

The best thing for being sad is to learn something. That is the only thing that never fails. You may grow old and trembling in your anatomies. You may lie awake at night listening to the disorder of your veins. You may miss your only love. You may see the world around you devastated by evil lunatics or know your honor trampled in the sewers of baser minds. There is only one thing for it, then: to learn. Learn why the world wags and what wags it. That is the only thing which the mind can never exhaust, never alienate, never be tortured by, never fear or distrust, and never dream of regretting. Learning is the thing for you.

—T. H. White, *The Once and Future King*

The advice of the wizard Merlin to the young King Arthur holds true for us commoners as well. Learning is the thing for all of us, at any age. It's not simply that learning is useful or practical. Learning is as essential to our minds as food is to our bodies. New ideas challenge and stimulate our intellects the way strenuous exercise challenges our muscles. In both cases, the result is growth.

An acquaintance of ours demonstrated recently how learning something new worked for her. When we asked her what was new in her life, Claire's eyes lit up. "Well, work has been slow," she began. We were puzzled—Claire is a freelance graphic designer, and when work is slow that usually means sleepless nights and worried looks.

"No . . . this time I'm glad!" she said, laughing at our expression of concern. "I decided I'd use the extra time as a gift, a chance to do something I really loved. As soon as I made that decision, I read about a college class on the history of cinema that was open to members of the community. The risk was minimal—I only had to sign up one week at a time—and I'd always loved movies, so I started going. And I was immediately hooked. For three hours a week each Wednesday, and for only five dollars a class, I hear a fascinating lecture on movies, art, and culture. I see one full-length movie and clips from many others. And I participate in rousing discussions with students half my age about cinematography, social realism, Expressionism—all kinds of subjects. I haven't had this much fun since I was in college myself! In fact," she added thoughtfully, "it's *more* fun now, because I don't have the pressure of taking tests and writing papers. I can just savor the knowledge." What's more, her discovery of classic movies is feeding Claire's imagination, giving her new ideas for her design work—an unexpected bonus.

Like Claire, we can all take delight in learning something new, at any age. Adult education, extension courses, and online learning bring formal education within the reach of virtually everyone in America. But learning can be informal, too: through a book group, a birdwatching outing, a docent-led tour of a museum exhibit. Stay attuned to opportunities to learn something new—to feed your brain new foods that satisfy old hungers.

Reclaim Conversation

One of the simplest, most accessible, and most rewarding of all intellectual pursuits is conversation. The gift of speech is uniquely human, and without good conversation our lives are impoverished. But truly enriching conversation is rare. When we're able to enjoy a real conversation—not gossip, not idle chat, not an exchange of monologues—we have good reason to be grateful.

Good conversation is rare because it's risky. It means listening attentively to ideas you may disagree with, and shaping your response in honest yet considerate terms. It means voicing opinions that may lead to disagreement. For many of us, disagreement equals dislike, and the fear of being disliked holds us back in our conversations. Instead, we neutralize our speech and limit it to trivial matters to avoid conflict. The result may be safe, but it isn't very satisfying. Argument is good, as long as one listens to the other person and responds appropriately.

It's entirely natural to want to be liked, but we need to watch out for carrying the desire too far. One of the stereotypes of the American character involves an excess of likability and a refusal of particularity and conflict: we turn into parodies of ourselves—smiling, earnest, generous, nice people who do terrible things quite inexplicably. As Daniel Goleman observes in his book *Emotional Intelligence,* people with good social skills but low self-respect often become "social chameleons [who] don't mind in the least saying one thing and doing another, if that will win them social approval."

If, on the other hand, we are set free from the fear of rejection—and from the desire to "win" arguments—we can feel secure in conversations, even when they turn confrontational. What matters is not being right but growing and deepening the relationship.

How do we enrich our conversational lives? By developing the art of listening, *really* listening, instead of merely waiting for our turn to talk.

After the tragedies of September 11, 2001, many people looked for ways to express their complicated feelings of grief, anger, fear, and confusion. We suspect that conversations—halting at first, then more eloquent—began to flourish in the aftermath.

In Seattle, a citywide network of "Conversation Cafes" sprang up, bringing strangers together to talk about important issues. In January, the city sponsored Conversation Week. The founder of the movement, Vicki Robin, a leader of the so-called voluntary simplicity movement, told the *New York Times* that she created the network "for people who sense there is something that needs to be done in our culture." She added, "We have pundits, we have opinion leaders, but that's not the culture reflecting upon itself."

Talk may be cheap, but its effects are priceless. Alan recalls seeing a poster about family life in his native England. In it, a parent is standing over a forlorn-looking teenager and saying, "What you need is a good listening to!" How true that is. We all need not a "talking to" but a "listening to"—an attentiveness, a respect for the things we say. What a gift! When you receive it, you can't help feeling grateful.

Practicing gratitude helps the mind open up to the big picture even as we battle with the particular issues that confront us day to day. Conversation helps us do both. It's not a mere decorative art but rather an essential skill for a society in which all of us can flourish. It not only keeps the mind open and supple, but also enables us to see the connections between people and things, which gives the mind satisfaction and delight. The natural response to the richness and wonder of existence is always gratitude.

Feed Your Mind

Feeding the mind is not a matter of stuffing it with information. Still less is it brainwashing with ideology. The true feeding of the mind can take place only where there is freedom to question, to reject or accept what is offered. In addition, the mind must be skilled and trained in discrimination. In fact, the mind is fed more through its questioning than by the information it seeks to sort out. As the mind's sympathies grow and deepen, so does its appetite.

Conscious feeding of the mind is no mere abstraction. Rather, it's a bit like putting on a play. We play out our thoughts and feelings in a great theater—an enormous "empty space." Into that empty space we place scenery and deploy actors. We design costumes and assign parts. We also choose the play being presented. What we put in that empty space is a matter of choice. If you don't choose your scenery and script, someone else (politicians, ideologues, religious leaders) will choose them for you. And you will find yourself an actor in someone else's play devised, say, by the Republicans or Democrats, the Catholics or the Protestants, the Israelis or the Palestinians, the fanatical Muslims or the moderate ones.

Now imagine there's another text—and the text is you. That text, with all its givens (where you were born, who your parents were, and so on), can be played in a variety of ways depending on how generously you feed your mind.

There's a paradox. For the mind to be well furnished, it needs to be emptied from time to time so that it can ask fresh questions. The theater director Peter Brook says he makes hundreds of sketches before the first rehearsal. "But I do this merely as an exercise, knowing that none of it is to be taken seriously the next day. . . . One needs to do the preparation in order to discard it, to build in order to demolish." The life of the mind is like that. Feed it. Be thankful.

Gratitude Practice: Learn New Things

1. Go to a book reading and force yourself to ask a question of the reader.
2. The next time you hear an opinion on the radio that makes you angry, go to the library or the Internet and read as much as you can about that opposing viewpoint. (Or write a "counterpoint" to the opinion, without resorting to angry language.)
3. Join a book group. Better yet, start one! Instead of reading current best sellers, invite the participants to read classics from ancient Greece, or from nineteenth-century England, or from the canon of great American literature.
4. Audit a class at a local university.
5. Memorize a poem. (Tip: Poems that rhyme are inherently easier to commit to memory.) The discipline of memorization gives

you a deep appreciation for words and their rhythms, and allows you to summon up a favorite passage any time, in any place. Choose a poet you've always admired, or select a topic such as, well, gratitude! Two to start: Edna St. Vincent Millay's "God's World," written when the poet was just 20 years old; and e.e. cummings's "i thank you god."

6. Write a letter of thanks to someone, living or dead, who has fed your mind in an important way. Karl Barth, the great Protestant theologian of the last century, provides an example with his letter to Mozart:

My dear Mozart:

What I thank you for is simply this: Whenever I listen to you, I am transported to the threshold of a world which in sunlight and storm, by day and by night, is a good and ordered world. Then, as a human being of the twentieth century, I always find myself blessed with courage (not arrogance), with tempo (not exaggerated tempo), with purity (not wearisome purity), with peace (not slothful peace). With an ear open to your musical dialectic, one can be young and become old, can work and rest, be content and sad: in short one can live.

Your own letter might be written to a favorite author or a college professor who gave you food for thought that continues to nourish you.

The goal of feeding your mind is not the empty calories of cleverness but the real nutrients of wisdom. So choose your meals well, and bon appetit!

14

Journeys of the Soul

It's good to have an end to journey toward; but it's the journey that
matters, in the end.

—Ursula K. LeGuin

In summer and winter we take vacations—trips that "vacate" our
minds and allow our bodies to rest and play. But autumn's crisp,
clear days stir a different yearning in us. It's the perfect time of year for
a *journey*: an adventure that alters our perceptions, raises our awareness, and fills us with gratitude for the world we inhabit.

A journey is different from a trip. The very word *trip* suggests its
alternate meaning of "trample" or "stumble." Like *travel,* which is
closely related to *travail,* a trip implies difficulties and hindrances,
staggering from baggage claim to shuttle bus to hotel room. But a *journey*—originally, the distance one could cover in a single day, the
French *jour*—evokes epic quests, soul-stirring adventures, and the
opportunity for self-discovery. When you take a trip you come home
weary with a suitcase full of dirty clothes. When you journey you
learn, as the naturalist John Muir did, that "going out . . . was really
going in." Or, as the thirteenth-century Sufi mystic Rumi wrote, "Journeys bring power and love back into you."

Symbolically, the fall is the time to slow down, to notice the vivid
colors of the leaves, the migrations of birds, the brilliance of sunlight
just before the days grow dark. It's a season that predisposes us to gratitude—for the natural beauty that surrounds us and for the unexpected
detours that can turn a trip into an odyssey of discovery. For the heart
of the journey is the wonder and gratitude in our own hearts.

Imagine the Journey

The first stage of any journey is dreaming about it. The idea for the journey may come from a long-held fantasy (wouldn't it be wonderful to sail to Tahiti?) or a sudden inspiration (a friend casually mentions that the Grand Canyon is beautiful in October, and you think, Why not?). The writer Kurt Vonnegut famously said that "peculiar travel suggestions are dancing lessons from God"—invitations to change the rhythm of your life. Will you say yes or no?

John recalls that his parents spent years preparing for their first trip to Europe and the Middle East. They read voraciously about Cromwell and King Richard, Aristotle and Moses. They knew where battles occurred, miracles happened, and divine births took place. They had walked the roads of Roman troops and the grand interiors of cathedrals in their minds before they ever left home.

For John's father, the dreaming-about-travel phase was by far the best part of the journey. He was distressed by the commercialization of sacred places and disappointed by the bad food they'd encountered, especially in London pubs. But John's mother had the opposite experience: She was enchanted to discover that the real sights and sounds were every bit as marvelous as the ones she'd imagined.

By all means, allow yourself to dream your journey. Steep yourself in travel literature, from *The Odyssey* to Jan Morris to Bruce Chatwin. Allow yourself to see places through others' eyes; give thanks that their descriptions have the power to move us still.

And then put away the books and begin your preparations. As Aldous Huxley observed, "For every traveller who has any taste of his own, the only useful guide-book will be the one which he himself has written."

Prepare Your Journey

Some people have an enviable gift for traveling light and on the spur of the moment. The rest of us, however, benefit greatly from preparing for—even rehearsing—our journey. Even this phase of our journey can be profoundly life changing.

Few of us will embark on a journey as epic as that of Dr. Jacques Pichard, the Swiss psychiatrist and explorer who assembled the first team to successfully go around the world in a balloon. The voyage took years of careful planning, all of which paid off when the team had to contend with unexpected crises.

But we all can learn from the careful preparations of seasoned journeyers. Knowing what you need—for your personal safety, your health, your comfort, and your appetite for adventure—is the first step in planning your journey. Anticipate those needs and plan and pack accordingly. (One veteran traveler of our acquaintance advises, "Lay out all your clothes and all your money—and then take half the clothes and twice the money.") And then accept that you cannot plan everything, for your journey or for your life. Getting lost, facing disappointment, and encountering the unfamiliar—from foreign languages to spartan accommodations—are all part of the journey of discovery.

In Pichard's words: "I have come back a different person. I realize what the limits are for controlling our lives. I know that I must learn to trust others to do anything of any scale. And I never can look at the sky without remembering how vast it is and how small and fragile we are."

Trip or Journey?

Recently we heard about two would-be journeys. The first was a gourmand's dream: an eighty-person tour of three-star restaurants in five European countries, where participants studied privately with chefs. Everything about the trip was first class; the cost came to $30,000 per person. The second trip was much more modest: a ten-day family excursion to Branson, Missouri, that shrine to country-and-western entertainment. The price for the whole family was under $4,000, shopping included.

Are these two experiences trips or journeys, and how do we know? One key criterion is motivation. Did the participants examine their reason for making the journey? Did the journey itself alter or challenge their motivations and expectations?

The answer to both questions, sadly, is no. The planning for both trips focused mostly on logistics: How will we get there? What will we eat? How long will we stay? A journey, on the other hand, requires us to answer very different questions: What do I need to know? What am I prepared to sacrifice? What do I hope to gain? A journey invades our imaginations, makes us sweat and blush in anticipation.

For the participants in the culinary and Branson trips, the idea was to get away, to be somewhere different—not an unreasonable goal in itself. But there was no built-in plan for introspection. Indeed, the focus was always external—on the sights, sounds, smells, and events at their destination. There was little time for reflecting, recording, and meditating on the experiences. The travelers returned home fatter and wearier, with bags full of mementos and dirty laundry. Trip over.

Trips are fine, even necessary. But they are not journeys.

What Kind of Journey?

You know you want a journey—a true odyssey for body and spirit. But you're not certain how to create one. Here are a few suggestions to point you on the path toward grateful journeying.

PHYSICAL CHALLENGE

A friend recently sent an e-mail describing his ascent to the summit of Mount McKinley in Alaska's Denali National Park, the highest point in North America. Our friend is in his mid-40s and fit, but not fanatically so. On the contrary, he's a soft-spoken investment banker who never takes himself too seriously.

He spent months planning for and dreaming about this trek. He knew there would be challenges, some severe; how would he handle them? What would he learn from them? Fortunately for his friends he wrote every day, introducing us to the other climbers and describing the hardships and the exhilaration so we could join in vicariously.

What does he bring home from these journeys? He knows more about what really matters. He grows in his self-knowledge, his appreciation for others, and his compassion. His wisdom widens and his insights deepen and, most delightfully for us, his sense of humor expands.

We don't need to challenge ourselves so strenuously to derive benefits from this type of journey. Hiking, biking, rafting, and canoeing trips can all qualify as physically demanding journeys. But we must plan to stretch, to plot and dream, to reach a bit deeper inside to discover what's there. Remember, getting lost, making mistakes, encountering risk, and learning to recover are all part of our learning journey.

ROMANTIC ADVENTURE

A hard-working executive in his mid-50s began planning years ago to sail around the world, including family and friends along the way. His dreams were saturated with the possibilities such a trip might bring: solidifying the family, renewing his marriage, rethinking his career.

Those of us who were privileged to track this journey on his web site could feel the progress each person enjoyed. This mythical journey had all of the elements of a dramatic odyssey: embarking with a dream in mind, visiting ports of call that evoke romantic images, following Shelley's search for his Grecian muse.

Our wiser, older mariner must now face his own change. Where does he fit in? He could hardly climb back into his old skin. How would he use his newly minted insights, his incipient wisdom?

One does not need an oceangoing yacht to have a mythic, romantic journey. It is not the scale of the journey but the way we approach it and carry it out that gives it meaning.

HISTORICAL RETRACING

A young couple spent two years preparing their daughters to tour the Civil War battlefields that had fascinated the father as a child. He tied the studies to genealogy so they would learn something about their ancestors. The family read stories, watched videos, went to movies, and studied maps—all before a single site had been visited. Once they arrived at the battlefields, they were able to vividly imagine the soldiers and their times. When they returned to school, the girls didn't write the usual "what-I-did-on-my-summer-vacation" stories. Instead, they were able to write eloquently about heroes, politics, cowardice, valor, and the sacrifices made by their own forebears. The whole family changed by experiencing themselves in this journey through fields of honor and horror.

Your own historical journey might involve retracing the steps of

Lewis and Clark, visiting the California Missions (spaced a day's walk apart—the perfect "journey" length), or even participating in an archeological dig. By traveling back in time, you'll experience a deep gratitude to those who came before us.

CULTURAL SATURATION

The book *A Year in Provence* was a witty account about living in a beautiful part of the world famed for good eating. But the real impact of the book was its deeper story, about a journey of personal self-discovery within a small French village.

When we uproot ourselves from familiar surroundings and plunge deeply into a new culture, we're forced to reexamine our habits, comforts, and customs. Gradually, we begin to see the world through a new lens—the lens of an expatriate resident rather than that of a tourist. There are great adventures of the heart to be realized by serving in medical missions to small Latin American villages, volunteering for the Peace Corps, or working in soup kitchens in the inner city. Consider following the migration of reindeer in Lapland, living with a Japanese family, or working on a project in a remote village in India.

ECOTOURISM

A century and a half ago, Ralph Waldo Emerson wrote, "At the gates of the forest, the surprised man of the world is forced to leave his city estimates of great and small, wise and foolish. The knapsack of custom falls off his back." It's harder today than it was in Emerson's time to experience this shedding of "civilized" ways. But thanks to a number of ecotourism outfitters, it's becoming more accessible.

John and his wife recently returned from a bike trip to Costa Rica, a country that has placed a high priority on the preservation of wild places. They had reveled in the beauty of the trails, beaches, and bike paths; the colors of exotic birds; the antics of howler monkeys.

Other eco-trips involve a commitment to study or repair endangered habitats. Consider joining a university research expedition or an Earthwatch trip that combines exotic vacation with spirit-nourishing journey.

Cultural Sojourns

When a major opera company announces an upcoming performance of Wagner's Ring Cycle, people around the world begin to make preparations for the cultural trek.

Devotees of James Joyce's writing tramp around Dublin each year in small private homages and elaborately planned fetes around "Bloomsday"—June 16, the date on which the entire novel *Ulysses* takes place.

A cultural journey can involve a week at a writing workshop or a month of playgoing in New York or London. It doesn't even need to involve a great deal of physical travel: A friend of ours takes two weeks off every spring to attend a film festival in her own city. "Standing in line with likeminded film buffs, watching movies from Poland and India and Spain, falling into excited conversations with perfect strangers—it's a wonderful way to travel around the world without having to set foot in an airport," she says. Each year, she "returns" from her film-festival break feeling stimulated and replenished.

Spiritual and Mental Pilgrimages

All journeys affect the spirit and the mind. Those journeys undertaken by pilgrims to visit holy places—Lourdes or Mt. Kailas in Tibet or the great Muslim shrines in the Middle East—can be profound and healing. But walking the labyrinth at Chartres in France or Grace Cathedral in San Francisco can also heal and transform. Attending a prayer session or engaging in a meditation retreat can be powerful journeys if entered well.

The "Roots" Journey

Amateur genealogy has never been more popular, and a journey to investigate your family origins can be powerfully life altering. Some people undertake these journeys alone; others make them multigenerational pilgrimages, which can enhance the sense of connection through blood and land. For Americans in particular, nearly all of whom are descended from immigrants, a roots journey has the potential of awakening a new consciousness about—and a new gratitude for—our personal histories.

Business and Family Travel

Where do business and family trips belong on a list of life-altering journeys? Simple: Any trip has the potential to become a journey if approached with an open heart and mind.

Our friend Cathy was once sent on a business trip to Iowa during Thanksgiving week. At first she felt sorry for herself—all alone in a strange place during a holiday devoted to family and friends. And Iowa! What could she possibly find of interest there? But from the start, she was surprised and delighted. Her business contacts turned out to be thoughtful, politically engaged, generous-spirited people who invited her into their homes and introduced her to their friends. One customer even invited her to Thanksgiving dinner. On a free afternoon, she took a leisurely stroll along one of the many trails converted from old railroad routes, and found herself reflecting on the spirit of this sturdy, unpretentious place. "Many Americans think of Iowa as 'flyover country,'" she says. "But to me it's truly heartland—a place where I discovered people and places with wonderful, caring hearts. That trip, which I almost didn't take, changed my life."

Anticipate Perils and Rewards

All adventure involves some risk, from missing a plane to coming down with *turista*. For some journeyers, the higher the risk, the greater the potential satisfaction.

Writer Tracy Johnston signed up for a rafting expedition on Borneo's Boh River despite her misgivings about the risks—and her husband's pleadings with her to stay home. "Long ago I realized a disconcerting truth about myself," she writes in *Shooting the Boh*, her account of the expedition. "I am by nature a passive person who likes excitement; a person with no magnificent obsessions who loves to participate in them. The best way to solve that contradiction, I'd discovered, was to go along on other people's rides, which is probably why I became a traveler and a journalist in the first place." The river trip ended up fulfilling her desire beyond her wildest imaginings. It became an odyssey of body and spirit.

Since September 11, 2001, all of us are much more keenly aware of the potential perils of travel. Yet we weigh the risks and rewards and make our plans accordingly. We would be wise to follow the sage words of a friend who travels for a living: "I like coping with the unknown, especially when I'm traveling in areas for the first time. But, especially where there are tourist warnings, don't push your luck. Use a guide who is well recommended. As tempting as it may be to wander into unknown areas, check first with reliable authorities."

How much risk do you need to feel alive? How much is too much to bear? How much safety do you require to feel confident? How can you strike a satisfying balance?

Embrace the Unexpected

In his book *In Search of Stones: A Pilgrimage of Faith, Reason and Discovery,* M. Scott Peck tells of a trip he and his wife, Lily, took through the British Isles, searching for Stone Age megaliths. The journey turned into a pilgrimage—an adventure of the spirit—because of the Pecks' ability to be open to chance encounters.

"We expected no stones this day," Peck writes of one such encounter. "Yet as we rounded a corner twenty miles inland on our way to Loch Ness, Lily suddenly screamed, 'There's one!' One, indeed. Smack in the middle of a large, golden valley meadow, silhouetted on all sides by mountains, stood a single fifteen-foot-high menhir, as proud and straight and strong as any that could ever be seen, dwarfing the sheep and cattle that grazed in its meadow. It was unmentioned in our guidebooks. It was not marked on our best map. There was no preparation for its simple magnificence. It was pure gift."

Are you grateful for the gifts that openhearted journeying can bring? Or disconcerted because they represented a detour from your itinerary?

Improvise

The best journeys are lived minute by minute, day by day. They are escapes from the usual, from routines and habits, from familiar places. Many purposes are served by adventuresome journeys: New lovers claim their romantic moments, wounded parties in a broken marriage try to forget and heal, bored housewives and tired executives attempt to renew flagging spirits.

As Dr. Samuel Johnson said, "The use of travel is to regulate the imagination by reality and instead of thinking how things may be, to see them as they are."

Keep a Record

"I never travel without my diary," Oscar Wilde had a character remark in *The Importance of Being Earnest*. "One should always have something sensational to read on the train."

Recording a journey means more than taking snapshots or lugging a video camera. The point is to make the act of recording as unintrusive as possible, so that the direct experience is always paramount.

You might try writing postcards—with brief descriptions of a place and its meaning for you—and sending them to yourself. When you return home, the postcards will serve as an illustrated journal.

Or pack a Polaroid camera and take instant photos of every stranger who helps you during your journey. Give a copy to each person as a thank you, and make one for yourself. Write the person's name, the date, and the encounter on the back of the photo. You'll have a meaningful "gratitude album" at the end of the journey.

Returning Home

Homer's *The Odyssey* is a tale of an epic journey, to be sure. But its point is the return of the hero, Ulysses, to the home he left years earlier. His homecoming is one of the most poignant scenes in the history of literature: Challenged by his suspicious wife, Penelope, who has nearly given up hope of seeing him again, Ulysses must pass a test to prove his identity.

When we return home from a journey, we might feel tested by the strangeness of once-familiar surroundings. We need to set aside time to sort out the experience. We might note how things may have changed while we were away. We might contrast what we have at home to what others have, and find new appreciation for the comforts and advantages we once took for granted. We may deepen our appreciation for our home itself. "The whole object of travel is not to set foot on foreign land," wrote the English novelist G. K. Chesterton. "It is at last to set foot on one's own country as foreign land." Journeying gives us the perspective to see familiar landscapes in fresh ways.

As we tell our friends about the journey, we need to pay close attention to what we're saying and what we're omitting. Which parts of the journey are most important in retrospect, and which recede into the background? What would you have changed about the journey, and why? How will this journey affect your future actions? You might, for example, choose to subscribe to an international newspaper or magazine to keep up with news in the places you visited. Or you might donate money to an organization that does good work there.

One way to think of a journey is to notice that all of our conscious plans have unconscious consequences. No matter what we set out to do, wherever we plan to go, what happens to us on the way is much more important and life changing than whatever our original intent may have been. "I met a lot of people in Europe," wrote the novelist James Baldwin. "I even encountered myself." If we journey in the right spirit, we may all have such a fortunate encounter.

15

Entering the Spirit

The glory of God is a human being fully alive.
—St. Irenaeus

You're Already on the Path

If you have been actively practicing gratitude as a stance toward life, matters of spirit will surface sooner or later. The very impulse to say thank you for the primary gift of life, and for all its subsequent gifts, suggests that we are in relationship with some infinitely generous source of all gifts in the universe. This doesn't mean that the person who lives gratefully must be a card-carrying believer, but it does mean that he or she will be open to what is loosely called the spiritual.

Religious scholar Karen Armstrong points out that we make a great mistake when we equate practicing faith with believing certain things about God or the sacred. A religious person is often called a "believer" and seen as one who has adopted certain correct ideas about the divine.

> Belief is . . . seen as the first and essential step of the spiritual journey. Before we embark on a religious life, which must make considerable demands on our moral, social, professional, and personal affairs, we think that we must first satisfy ourselves intellectually that there is a God or that the truths of our particular tradition—Jewish, Christian, Muslim, Buddhist, Hindu, or whatever—are

valid. It seems pointless to make a commitment unless we are convinced about the essentials. In our modern, scientific world, this makes good, rational sense: First you establish a principle, and then you apply it. But the history of religion makes it clear that this is not how it works. To expect to have faith before embarking on the disciplines of the spiritual life is like putting the cart before the horse.

Armstrong points out, "In all the great traditions, prophets, sages, and mystics spent very little time telling their disciples what they ought to *believe*." They were invited to trust that, "despite all the tragic and dispiriting evidence to the contrary, our lives did have some ultimate meaning and value. You could not possibly arrive at faith in this sense before you have lived a religious life. Faith was thus the fruit of spirituality, not something that you had to have at the start of your quest."

You don't have to share formal beliefs to explore a spiritual path. In fact, we're suggesting that in practicing gratitude you're already on the path. Here are some new ways to think about it that will take your gratitude practice in deeper and more satisfying directions.

What Is Spirituality?

So what is "spirituality"? It's one of those umbrella terms that covers a multitude of experience. Think of it, for a moment, as something neutral. Think of it as a way of arranging the bits and pieces of our lives (like a big jigsaw puzzle), then gluing them together to make a picture. Spirituality in this neutral sense is how we choose to arrange the pieces and glue them together.

To find out a person's spiritual take on life, ask yourself: how have they arranged their pieces and what kind of glue do they use? One person might arrange the pieces to show how smart they are and use the art of put-down to glue it all together. Another might arrange the pieces to show how victimized they are. The glue of entitlement and resentment is very effective. So there are a lot of false spiritualities out there—damaging ways of making sense of your life.

Spirituality of the Marketplace

Let's look at one current example of spirituality in this way. Some would suggest the dominant spirituality of our age—the Zeitgeist—is the spirit of the global market, with economic exchange as the glue holding the world together. The jigsaw puzzle called "the Market" makes a picture people find attractive. It promises a great deal. The spiel goes something like this: the Market makes the world a rational place. With its global dimensions and rational efficiency, this belief system could wipe away every tear and deliver the gold to every believer. Leave the Market alone (free from government interference) and it will generate wealth for all. The Market delivers what church, temple, and synagogue have failed to deliver: the Kingdom of God on earth.

The new priesthood is made up of economists and social scientists who can interpret the market. It's a very persuasive and powerful religion with many followers. It offers a vigorous spirituality—a coherent arrangement of the pieces and some very tough glue.

Some have even been able to splice the Market view with their peculiar form of piety. As described in *Harper's* magazine, one couple had a brochure printed for guests in their home to explain how God guided them in the choice of furnishings for their "big, beautiful house." "As we took several pleasure trips around the world, the Lord God would put into our hearts to buy certain pieces of furniture for our future house. Our favorite place was Italy . . . In China we acquired very good buys. My husband said, 'Okay, we are here in Hong Kong, so buy all the Oriental rugs you need for our dream house,' I prayed to God for direction and bought the most beautiful floral rugs I'd ever seen."

In this chapter, we're concerned with something deeper than a shopping spree confused with a relationship with God. What kind of picture does each of us construct from all those pieces of puzzle we find lying all around us? In the Introduction we quoted the poet John Ciardi: "We are what we do with our attention." We have a choice where to place our attention. And we must be concerned for the truth of the picture of the world we choose.

The great religious traditions have certain things in common with regard to the nature of true spirituality. For one thing, true spirituality, as a method, often works negatively by telling us about dead ends rather than right paths. Let's try to identify some of the marks of true spirituality.

The Art of Self-Simplification

One of the benefits of cultivating a practice of gratitude is that life—on the other side of complexity—gets simpler. Spirituality is the art of self-simplification, pulling ourselves together. We return to the theme of integrity—not the moralistic kind, but the kind when all the bits and pieces of our lives are in touch with each other. The fully human life is one in harmony with the world (you don't have to use the word "God"), with others, and with your deepest self.

In the Christian mystical tradition there are three disciplines for self-simplification as a way of enjoying the world. They are prayer, almsgiving, and fasting. These disciplines, in turn, are ways of clarifying our approach to three basic relations: to God (prayer); to others (almsgiving: the traditional works of mercy such as giving food to the hungry, caring for the sick, visiting those in prison); and the self (fasting).

These disciplines are pursued for the sake of freedom, though they don't sound like liberation. In fact, they used to be called mortifications—ways of dying. But it would be a mistake to switch off and refuse to think about them, because the goal behind them was a fuller and freer life. After all, one of the signs that we are finally growing up is that we can delay gratification and give up something good (ice cream) for something better (a healthier body). The old disciplines are worth looking at closely. They can be a way of sorting out what's really life bearing and what's really death dealing. What passes for life can be deadly and what looks deadly could bring new life.

One way is to think of all the things that we think will bring us a happy life but in fact bring enslavement and misery. Most addictions start off with the promise of freedom and deeper experience of life. What were once pleasures become habits that are hard to shake and offer diminishing returns. What we once enjoyed and felt free to do or not to do becomes the source of guilt or shame.

The fifteen-year-old daughter of a friend who is struggling with her own definitions of spirituality was having a particularly hard time at Lent. The message that got through to Grace about the practice of "giving something up" for Lent was, "I suck; beat me!" A college-age friend of the family responded with these comments, which hint at how spiritual disciplines can be liberating:

> I was thinking that, perhaps, Lenten devotions are like fasting. Fasting is not good. Eating is good (and not just enjoyable, but good). But fasting makes us aware of our desire for something good. It allows some degree of empathy for all the people in the world who desire good things but don't have them. But fasting also reminds us of how passionately we desire the good things we get every day. It reconnects us with our most ordinary, and perhaps most passionate desires. Like desire for God. God is first among the good things we get to enjoy. And we've got God all the time. But I don't really notice my desire for God all that often. Finding some way to reconnect with those ordinary and passionate desires could provide a way to *realize* the most passionate, pressing and ordinary of our desires.

It's not much fun to live always with a deficit self and be on the treadmill of improvement all the time. But the goal is to ripen rather than become flawless. The American Buddhist abbess Pema Chodron puts it well: "It's about befriending who we already are."

The fourth-century humanist mystic Gregory of Nyssa tells us that there is nothing more important than this befriending. He saw life as an unending progress of discovering how God is at work among humanity always calling us into friendship, and sin as refusal to keep on growing in this discovery:

> This is true perfection: not to avoid a wicked life because we fear punishment, like slaves; not to do good because we expect repayment, as if cashing in on the virtuous life by enforcing some business deal. On the contrary, disregarding all those good things which we hope for and which God has promised us, we regard falling from God's friendship as the only thing dreadful, and we consider becoming God's friend the only thing truly worthwhile.

Spirituality as Ripening

As Doug Shadel and Ellen Stephen put in their book *Vessel of Peace: Towards Spiritual Freedom,* spirituality is a matter of ripening: "A mature human being is created to 'ripen' in several ways: in consciousness, in the capacity to choose well, and how to love well." Put another way, our tasks are: "Staying awake, trying to see things clearly, and trying to grapple with the question of how to accept the unacceptable."

Think of the three ways of ripening: being awake, choosing wisely, and learning to love. It is not difficult to see how they are related to the three disciplines of self-simplification. Prayer is a way of becoming more awake to what the world has to offer. Choosing well requires self-knowledge. And loving deeply requires relating to others in community and communion.

Years ago the Canadian Jesuit Bernard Lonergan formulated four spiritual imperatives that also echo the path of self-simplification:

- Be attentive
- Be intelligent
- Be reasonable
- Be in love

"In the end," writes St. John of the Cross, "we shall be examined in love." All human beings are called to being in love. This is the lesson we have to learn in the end, embracing lovers of all persuasions— believers, half-believers, and unbelievers alike. Life and love cannot be possessed or clutched at. "Be in love" is the imperative. Mary Oliver's poem "Wild Geese" speaks the same truth from an ecological or pantheistic point of view:

> You do not have to be good.
> You do not have to walk on your knees
> for a hundred miles through the desert, repenting.
> You only have to let the soft animal of your body
>   love what it loves.
> Tell me about despair, yours, and I will tell you mine.

Meanwhile the world goes on. . . .
Meanwhile the wild geese, high in the clean blue air,
are heading home again.
Whoever you are, no matter how lonely,
the world offers itself to your imagination,
calls to you like the wild geese, harsh and exciting—
over and over announcing your place
in the family of things.

The Challenge of Spiritual Maturity

What might spiritual ripeness look like? In the end, life is a matter of
allegiances. What have you chosen to serve? The poet Rilke gives us a
clue when he wrote, "Where I am folded in upon myself, there I am a
lie." We fool ourselves into thinking that we can make ourselves
immune from the natural and inevitable failures that are part of our
living in history—in a particular time and place. There is no cure for
impermanence but there is an implicit adventure in being alive. We
sabotage ourselves with our irrational need to be eternally competent
or when we close off parts of ourselves to protect us from pain.

The cost of being awake is an awareness of the brokenness of the
world as well as its glory. As Buddhism tells us, to be conscious is to be
sad. There is no escape from the messiness of human history, the
sense of darkness and inferiority in individual lives. When we wake up
to gratitude, we also wake up to the stabilizing delusions of human
life. Everything we hide from must come out—collectively as well as
personally.

Gratitude becomes more and more important because it guards
against despair and disillusionment. We begin to appreciate that
everyone is in the same vulnerable boat and, as a psychiatrist friend
tells us, "there is no such thing as a grown-up person." We can take
heart! Gratitude helps us to be tender towards others and ourselves.

We glibly talk about someone being in denial. But it isn't easy to
give up this coping strategy when things get tough. Spiritually mature
humans face experiences of loss and limitation without resorting to
strategies of denial. Their lifeline is gratitude. If we cannot make this

passage, we may turn to violence. Unless we find ways to work through a terrible wrenching sadness, we turn on others.

When we talk about matters of spirit we are talking about being in touch with a disturbing psychic weakness through which the spirit reaches us and breathes new life and courage into us. This power in weakness is usually suppressed. Who needs it? And who, in their right mind, would be grateful for it? Whether we like it or not, the suppressed and unlived parts of our lives will eventually burst out of hiding and surprise us—sometimes violently and messily—like a pressure cooker exploding in the kitchen. The suppressed life will come out.

It's hard to be grateful for what simply *is* when the form of what *is* appears intransigent and even horrible. This is where the vast treasures of the spiritual traditions can help us. Those disciplines can teach us how to wait in the darkness for a deeper reality to appear, so that what we thought was impossible or unbearable takes on a new form.

Matters of spirit are not merely personal. They are political and social, too. Think of the repressed anger in people slighted and abused because of the color of their skin, their sex, or the way they talk. Such anger explodes with terrible social consequences. As we write, the world is still reeling from the threat of terrorist attacks. The more thoughtful among us (without denying the horrors of terrorism) are wondering what we might have done differently to ward off the hatred and resentment that occasioned the attacks. Dante writes of the sullen lazy smoke in the hearts of the damned. Our sullenness tends towards disengagement. We detach ourselves (or try to) from the world and from each other. In an essay, David Whyte reminds us that "without soulful entanglement with the world we experience a poverty that no amount of material reward or recognition can ameliorate."

We know that we are relatively rich and privileged. Anyone reading this book is one of the lucky ones. We wonder why the world is so unstable. For some it is indeed the best of times, for most it is the worst. But we did not choose the place, time, and circumstances of our birth. The question now is how should we live responsibly, generously, and gratefully. We are called to join the grown-ups. When Michael Ramsey (the late Archbishop of Canterbury) was asked, "How would you define wisdom?" he replied, "I should say wisdom is the ability to cope." It's a modest answer, and the absence of grandiosity gives it authenticity.

Keep Your Sense of the Ridiculous

One byproduct of practicing gratitude is humor. Laughter is a great antidote to resentment and anger. Spirituality without humor is priggishness, and there's an important link between comedy and religion. Authority always needs to be challenged—even mocked and attacked—so that the spiritual experience can be deepened and serve the interests of freedom. Remember, at the heart of true spirituality is love, and love requires freedom.

Proper reverence includes a sense of the ridiculous. Playwright Christopher Fry wrote, "Comedy is an escape not from truth, but from despair: a narrow escape into faith." And Bertholt Brecht insists: "One may say that tragedy deals with the sufferings of mankind in a less serious way than comedy." Shocking? Yes, but true. Comic vision does not give suffering and evil a dangerous romantic grandeur or an inevitable dominance. The last word isn't the worst word. Joy is a very serious business! A human being is *homo ludens,* a playing and playful animal.

We should be merciful to ourselves. For millions of people, it takes a great deal of quiet courage to get up in the morning and not despair or surrender to resentment in the face of powerlessness. A sense of the ridiculous helps us move on beyond the resentment and the cynicism.

Humor is also important in the face of evil. Evil is not trivial, but an old tradition has it that the devil cannot bear to be laughed at. Humor is a weapon against the darkness. It can help us identify "the truth about lies" in our personal, social, and political lives.

True spirituality as a process of self-simplification and truth telling for the sake of love offers an antidote to the consumerist, power-driven images that dominate our culture. Being open to gratitude is a way of being subversive and rebellious in a culture that too easily cheapens us.

When John Robinson, an English Anglican bishop, was close to death from cancer, he said in a farewell sermon, "Christians above all are those who should be able to bear reality and show others how to bear it." We might say that all people who are on a true spiritual path are growing in ways to bear reality and show others the way.

✧

Gratitude Practices: Spiritual Ripeness

1. Practice saying thank you—that old exercise of counting your blessings—every day, preferably before you even get out of bed. Try beginning the day with a sense of gratitude.

2. Set aside time (start modestly: say, ten minutes) to sit still and practice being awake and aware. Just sitting still is harder than most of us think. And sitting still while focusing our attention is even harder. Be patient with yourself; notice how the mind wanders and won't stay at rest. Just notice it without judging yourself.

3. Write down the main points of your actual, functioning spirituality (not what you believe would sound good about you). Think about how you have arranged the jigsaw puzzle of your life and glued them together. (One way to find out how your spirituality actually works is to ask yourself, "What would have to be taken away for my life to begin to fall apart?" The third glass of wine? The car? The job? News that I had cancer? Divorce? Aerobics? It can be anything from the deeply important to what others may consider trivial. Your answer will give you a clue to what drives you.)

4. List three things you can do right now to simplify your life.

5. "Be in love" is the supreme imperative. When did you feel passionately, irresistibly drawn to anyone or anything? Try giving certain things your full attention—start with a flower, your cat, the sunset; you can graduate to friends and loved ones.

6. Perhaps the biggest obstacle to growing spiritually is our wounded emotional life with its cravings. Roger Walsh in his book *Essential Spirituality* suggests several exercises to reduce our cravings. He quotes Mohammed: "Free yourself from greed, for greed itself is an impoverishment." It's a long process but

our attachments can weaken over time and our compulsions become less potent. Walsh advises that the first thing we could do is to recognize pain as feedback. Practice noticing when you're experiencing fear or anger and stop and see if there's an attachment behind the negative emotion. Slowly you will be able to redirect your life.

❧

PART IV

Winter

Living into Gratitude

Tim, a smart, thoughtful computer programmer in his late thirties, is typical of recent generations of Americans—rejecting his family's religion because it failed his intellectual needs, subscribing wholeheartedly to the twentieth century's faith in the individual self and the power of science and rationality. He felt exiled from any sense of community, having been transplanted several times as a child and moving around even more as an adult.

In college he discovered his love and aptitude for space, science, and computers. The latter became his career, and at age 23 he married a fellow space enthusiast. "But I was still smoking dope, having started in high school, and I was very angry without really knowing it. I think it had to do with feeling cut off from my spiritual self, though I didn't know it then." He took it out on his wife, he says, and when they divorced she gave him an earful about the person he had become.

"That got me into treatment. I stopped smoking pot and started looking at the underlying problems in therapy. That's when I turned back towards religion. First I went to a Unitarian church where I could be an atheist. And I liked Buddhist meditation because I could do the spiritual practice without having to accept any doctrines."

In the early 1990s he moved to the Bay Area in California to get serious about his career, and cofounded a software company. Excited to be using his talents to the utmost, he worked seven days a week for years, growing even more isolated and arrogant. His company merged with a German firm, and in Berlin he met Greta, now his fiancée.

When Greta and I went on vacation in Turkey, it was a real awakening for me. I had the sudden realization: "Here I feel rich." And that meant I expected people to treat me a certain way. But other experiences there hinted that my spiritual nature was aching to get out. In a chapel near Ephesus I felt a powerful shock. I thought, "I've just completely wasted my life, being pissed off at people, playing all these selfish roles, and I don't have much time left." And one day in the Blue Mosque in Istanbul, the muezzin started calling, and it just struck me: "Oh, this is why religion is important, to live your spirituality in some kind of form! You need something concrete to practice."

When we came back to the States, we started looking for a church where we felt at home, intellectually and spiritually. We found one—more than that, I found a calling I never dreamed was in me, to work in a community.

I became quite involved in the life of the congregation, serving as a deacon and at our food pantry. For years I'd always found an excuse not to do things like this. Now I had the irresistible feeling: "Stop making excuses and just go." I was afraid, because I felt so different from the people who come there to get free groceries. I thought they'd be angry with me. But the experience was one of total welcoming. And realizing that I could be useful was exciting.

Why was it such a big deal? The best answer I could come up with was that the church is a way of learning how to pray in community, and the food pantry is a way of learning how to serve the community. I'm sort of a natural for this kind of work, it turns out— much to my surprise.

In this last part of the book, we'll find out, like Tim, what happens when we let gratitude shape our lives and our stories, when we discover that making and sustaining connections is work to be undertaken as seriously as any career. In winter we take our practice of gratitude out into the world, into our life in community: celebrating feasts, deepening relationships, serving as both host and guest at the table of blessings. And we take the practice deeper inward, with the ultimate challenge of being grateful for our mortality.

Practicing gratitude is the journey of a lifetime—as we said back at the beginning, our practice will always be in some stage of summer or autumn or winter. But we have the assurance that spring—those astounding, evergreen, ever-fresh moments of clarity and wonder—is always in wait.

16

The Host and the Guest

Both abundance and lack exist simultaneously in our lives, as
parallel realities. . . . [W]hen we choose not to focus on what is
missing from our lives but are grateful for the abundance . . . the
wasteland of illusion falls away and we experience Heaven on earth.
— SARAH BAN BREATHNACH

A contented heart is a continual feast.
— PROVERB

W inter is a season for feasting, for gathering around the table with
those we care for to celebrate life's gifts. It's the time of our
wonderful holiday feasts: Christmas or Chanukah or Kwanzaa or the
other December feasts, which all derive from celebrations of the solstice—the return of the light, of the lengthening days. Special food is
prepared; hearth and hall are lovingly decorated; far-flung family
members and friends reunite; gifts are exchanged (sometimes even
meaningful ones). And among Christians, at least, a great gift is welcomed joyfully year after year.

St. Francis of Assisi found in the humble birth of Jesus a touching
image of God's hospitality. God, the universal host, thought Francis,
came as a vulnerable guest into the world. He saw the crib in the stable
as a sign of God embracing our poverty—both the literal poor and the
poverty of spirit that makes us realize we are, finally, as vulnerable as
any baby. We too are guests just passing through, and we're called to
be hosts to each other.

As Timothy Radcliffe points out in *I Call You Friends,* this vision of Francis's was extraordinary in the Renaissance world of the thirteenth century, "with its new frescoes, new exotic consumer goods, its new urban civilization, its mini-globalization." Sounds a bit like our own time! Our attempts at true hospitality can be pretty thin, since our appreciation of who is our neighbor has worn thin too. A lot of us don't even know who lives next door or down the hall, and much of our entertaining is prompted not so much by joy as by a sense of obligation: It's expected of us. But when we get in touch with our own vulnerability, there's a chance that our circle of sympathy might grow larger, might include more and more people. As we come to know our shared frailty, we have the chance to live more gratefully and gracefully.

Welcoming the Stranger

Alan recalls a recent dinner when he and his wife welcomed among their guests three friends who brought hard tales to the table. One had just been diagnosed with Parkinson's, the husband of another told us his wife had Alzheimer's, and the third was coping with the effects of a minor stroke. "We all felt the chill wind of mortality but also felt grateful for the countless times we had celebrated our friendship over good meals. Those who were suffering now had listened to our hard stories in times past. We appreciated this occasion to give them even a temporary refuge at our table."

Ritual gatherings around food, whatever time of year they are enacted, highlight the importance of hospitality, at our tables and in our hearts. When the world was a dangerous place for nearly everyone and people were much more dependent on each other, strict traditions grew up around hospitality; they still survive in some cultures. It can be a serious crime to refuse help to a neighbor or to betray someone who has sat at your table. In places where life is harsh you'll still find such traditions.

Isolated monasteries and other religious houses are among such places. When Alan visited the monastery of St. Macarius in the Egyptian desert a few years ago, the monk who welcomed him said, "We welcome you as an angel of God," adding with a twinkle in his eye, "just in case!" You never know who your guest might be. And you never know when you might be in need of a welcome.

True hospitality calls on us to be open to the surprising presence of the stranger—from whom we may receive surprising gifts. Each of us is born to this dual role: to be a host welcoming others to the table, and to be a guest grateful for hospitality offered. Each role brings its own joys and obligations. Our natural inclinations vary: for some of us, it's harder to be a guest. For others it's harder to give hospitality. But when we consciously practice both, we see most clearly the powerful two-way dynamic of gratitude.

We Are How We Eat

Food is a source of deep human pleasure. Gathering around food in the company of others feeds the soul as well as the senses. After the gift of existence itself, nothing elicits gratitude more profoundly than food—the thing that sustains life from first breath to last. We eat because we must. We eat because it gives us joy. But to rejoice in food we need to go without it for a time. Living well requires balance: a cycle of feasting and fasting; the feast is no reward unless preceded by the fast. It's one of life's great dualities: a seesaw between necessity and delight.

For as long as we know, humans have recognized that food comes to us through some kind of sacrifice: plants or animals being harvested or killed and consumed, then mysteriously transformed into our own substance. This was a miracle that needed to be shared and talked over and incorporated into the spiritual life of every human tribe. No wonder so many cultures have evolved rituals and mysteries around food. Celebrations for the bounty of the hunt or harvest, laws about what things can be eaten (and when), and prayers of thanksgiving for the blessings of food are as old as humankind.

The intensity of grateful feeling with which a starving person receives food isn't likely to be experienced in middle-class, well-fed lives. Most of us know that people in many parts of the world respond to the gift of food on this level, but we can only imagine it. Someone who becomes lost for days on a wilderness hike might approach understanding. Or we might get a hint when we forget to eat because we are frantically busy, or ill, or grieving, or otherwise emotionally distraught. Of course, food always tastes exceptionally good when we are keenly hungry.

But since we are rarely deprived of food, our boundless appreciation for it comes mostly from other sources. Sheer sensual pleasure, for one. Some believe the most transporting pleasures are available to those with the most educated palates, but is that really true? We can all remember times when the simplest food struck us as the best thing we ever ate: a slice of crisp, juicy apple; a bowl of grains; a fish just out of the water and grilled over a fire. Our grateful feelings about food have so much to do with associations of place and time and the people we eat with, and the quality of attention we give our food.

Think about the way we treat food! Usually it's much the same as how we treat life, how we treat people. We sometimes gobble it unconsciously: where did that packet of chips go? What about that bar of chocolate? Sometimes we savor the omelet, grateful for the soothing warmth and herbal aroma of each bite. Like good lovemaking, a good meal should be enjoyed as slowly as possible.

Nothing affects our feelings about food as strongly as the social circumstances of eating. When we feel welcomed and safe and comfortable at the table, food tastes good, and special fondness attaches to food we associate with exceptional hospitality. A young friend traveling in England got in a car wreck in the Lake District and was taken in by a family from Liverpool on holiday in a rented house. She spent a week with them, amusing their children with cards on rainy days. "Mrs. Harris would bring a huge mug of steaming, strong, milky tea up to my room every morning," she recalls. "I loved that tea." What memorably flavored the tea was Mrs. Harris's generous hospitality.

Conversely, children who grow up with tension and acrimony at the dinner table are far more likely to hate certain foods they associate with childhood and sometimes develop eating disorders, studies show. And the most elegant dishes can turn to dust in our mouths if we feel rushed by our host or betrayed by the dining companions with whom we sat down in trust.

What Is a Feast?

Making a feast with our fellows raises many issues: of appetite and restraint, of attention and appreciation, of gratification and its delay. Guests as well as hosts have their rights and duties, chief among them being to practice the art of conversation, of being a good companion. (A com*pan*ion, after all, is someone with whom we share our bread: *panis* in Latin). There are right and wrong ways of dressing for a dinner party. Dressing for the occasion is a way of showing affection and respect for one's hosts. Discovering what it means to be both guest and host involves many skills of human interaction. Sharing food offers a prism through which to look at the whole of our lives.

What is a feast? It can be any kind of meal at all, enjoyed in the company of others as we celebrate that companionship. A feast is an orange shared with fellow hikers or a wedding banquet for several hundred. All kinds of outdoor feasts are possible: urban-park picnics, a tailgate party, ballpark hot dogs, a beach clambake. Some feasts are clearly seasonal, with food to match: Fourth of July barbecues, Easter Sunday dinners, a holiday open house. Some honor an individual upon a graduation or a retirement, or at a wake.

Cultural and religious festivals give rise to an endless variety of feasts, from the Chinese New Year banquet to the Passover Seder to Little Italy's raucous Feast of San Gennaro, a multi-day street party in lower Manhattan. (Each Catholic saint has his or her own "feast day," many with special dishes associated with them.)

Two people can make a feast: a couple, a pair of old friends, a parent making special time for a child. At the other end of the scale, communal feasts organized by large family clans, social clubs, or churches turn many participants into both host and guest.

Potlucks are a wonderful kind of feast, where again the host responsibilities are shared. They can range from highly organized—a gathering of amateur chefs eager to try out their latest recipes on cohorts, with one mastermind of the menu—to events where everyone trusts fate that all the dishes won't turn out to be desserts. (Usually it works out fine.) John recalls his parents hosting potlucks during the Depression as a way for neighbors to share scarce resources and console each other in dismal days. Each person brought something and all offerings were honored. Often these affairs were a dignified means of augmenting the diets of the less fortunate.

Then there's the traveling feast: where a host brings food, comfort, and companionship to "guests" who are ill, newly delivered of infants, or bereaved. Some do this on their own; some through their churches; some through community food programs like San Francisco's Project Open Hand, which ministers to AIDS patients. A friend of ours relates how, after her father's recent death, a friend who had just lost his partner to cancer brought her a big box of chocolates with the instructions to "take five or six and call me in the morning." That was a feast!

Some meals are definitely not feasts: the performance review lunch, the break-up dinner in a public place, the Golden Globe Awards, and any corporate rubber-chicken banquet. Sometimes we find ourselves at a meal when we would rather be somewhere else, like Alice at the Mad Hatter's tea party. A relaxing meal with people we trust is an antidote to the madness of the world. At Mad Hatter's party you weren't allowed to sit still for long. When you have to eat with March Hares and Mad Hatters, the best thing to do is to put your head down, eat as fast as possible, and escape at the earliest opportunity. There is no sense of being a guest.

Making Conversation

The only real requirement for a feast is a conscious intent to enjoy and celebrate fellowship, the indispensable connections that season our lives and make food taste better. Ideally the only entertainment should be conversation, unless live music is an important theme. Plato used the word "dinner-party" (*symposium*) to describe what life was really about: a party where we tell each other stories about the meaning of our longing. His great work titled *Symposium* is the record of a conversation over dinner.

Fine fare and drink are the time-honored fuel of good conversation. Think of those memorable meals when the conversation took off and you were transported through the medium of good food and wine to a place within yourself that you rarely visit, or to an unknown land brought to life by a companion's eloquent description. Think of less grand occasions—a long evening over beer and pizza when time slowed down and the smallest, silliest detail of life was worth lingering over. Or when a reminiscence sent the whole table into howls of helpless laughter.

The food for a feast should preferably be prepared by loving hands, but there's no rule that good takeout, leftovers, or a restaurant meal can't be a feast, if consumed in the right spirit. Cocktails and especially good wine can warm a gathering and add a ceremonial glow, as long as they don't take over.

There are many ways to create a symposium. You can try something as simple as turning off the TV, if you and your mate have grown accustomed to having it on during dinner, and deliberately catching up with each other on your days. Some families with children take turns at letting each sit at the head of the table and choose what to talk about, or a child is informally honored for an accomplishment at the meal. You can organize your own symposium around any theme you choose: a book, a movie, an event in the news, travel. Sometimes the food can reflect the theme: a group invited to a friend's home for dinner shared a passion for Hawaii and its culture, and the menu was designed around this.

Banquet or Fortress?

Many religious traditions imagine life as a great banquet to which everyone is invited. A Celtic vision of the afterlife has heaven flowing with beer. The Christian mass, the Chinese communal meal, the Japanese tea ceremony are all different ways to celebrate life as a banquet. There's a famous Chinese story in which heaven and hell are nearly identical, each overflowing with sumptuous and plentiful food. All the guests are provided with chopsticks six feet long. The only difference between the two places is that in hell people try in vain to eat on their own with the enormous chopsticks; they find it impossible to put food in their own mouths and they go hungry. In heaven, they feed each other.

A friend of John's divides people into two types: those who have a banquet mentality and those with a fortress frame of mind. The fortress type finds it hard to be thankful because gratitude requires, in some measure, the gift of our unguarded selves. "When I am with friends, especially over dinner," says Alan, "I become more trusting, more expansive, more capable of taking risks. I also find that I am more inclined to pick up the tab in a restaurant! I become more generous, less fearful. I can afford to reveal my unguarded self. I am safe enough to experience the glory of gratitude."

We have met those committed to the banquet of life in all sorts of places: in artists' studios, on the meanest of streets, in offices and boardrooms. For them life is a feast and everyone is both host and guest. Many of us have travel stories of being welcomed and fed by those much poorer than ourselves—like Samir, the Cairo taxi driver, who took our friend Jim to a dive in that city for "the kind of food I like." Jim had hired Samir for the day; they had got on well and Samir wanted to say thank you. At first Jim was terrified by the thought of food poisoning, but he got over it. "I had the best time in a place I would never have found on my own. Samir invited me generously into a whole new world."

Contrast this with the world most of us inhabit in the affluent and individualistic West, where few seem to have something to live for outside ourselves. Too often life is not a banquet to which everyone is invited. It's more like a cafeteria with not enough seats and limited servings. Ironically, it is often the affluent who have a mentality of scarcity. They give less to charity, percentagewise, than their poorer counterparts and tend to fear that their resources will run out before they die. The heart freezes in its fortress, the soul in perpetual winter.

Terence Rattigan's play *Separate Tables* is about a group of sad, isolated people living in a pretentious, slightly run-down seaside hotel where the dining room is proud to offer the amenity of eating at separate tables. As the play unfolds, that system breaks down and the guests begin to see how unnatural is their separation from each other. One of the things gratitude teaches us is that true security is found in social solidarity rather than in isolated achievement.

We have often mentioned our frustration with time. It goes too fast. There's not enough of it. We try to cram too much into it. This is part of the fortress mentality. In contrast, the give and take of hospitality takes time. Good hosts don't hurry or bully their guests. And good guests take time to express appreciation of the efforts made on their behalf. We complain of "information overload." Worse, we confuse information with communication and fail to see that we need more than communication. We need affiliation, the first step to building community.

We need ways to share the banquet—the opportunity and privilege of welcoming others to the table. Without a vision of a respectful, supportive community there's no way our thinking and feeling can mature into grateful, compassionate action. Practicing gratitude helps us see each other as hosts and guests.

Make a Place at the Table

Our shared need for food makes us vulnerable. It reveals our fragility, our subjection to necessity. And because of this, food becomes one of the ways we demonstrate our care and love for each other. Gratitude is a way of being introduced to our obligations and duties. What do we owe each other? What might it mean—out of a sense of gratitude, not guilt—to widen the circle of our hospitality?

From a spiritual point of view, we all want an invitation to the banquet of life, a place at the table. There is something isolatingly terrible about not being welcome—like poor kids sticking their faces right up against the window to watch the people feasting inside. Like Oliver Twist daring to ask for more.

In most homes, meals are served family-style, and the common meal of the Christian feast or the Jewish Sabbath has much the same feeling of inclusion. A shared meal is one of the ways in which the saints understood heaven. In fact, reality is by definition something shared. A purely private reality would be hell. Sharing is a natural consequence of seeing the world as it really is. As the spiritual maxim goes, "Being is communion."

Our individuality is a precious gift and the drive for individual achievement has served us well, but we can go too far and find ourselves shipwrecked on a lonely island. What sort of person do we want to be? It's hard to imagine anyone wanting to remain frozen in a winter of isolation, but many of us seem to find ourselves outside the door where the banquet is going on. Don't we long for companionship? Wouldn't we like a place at the table? Whom do you want to hang out with? Do we want the fellowship of those mad and wonderful people who risk caring about the world, who understand that to know the world is to love it?

The grateful heart holds a vision of common good and shared responsibility. This banquet mentality sees others not just as some kind of instrument to further our projects or populate our schemes. Those others are our neighbors and helpers—sharers "on a par with ourselves in the banquet of life to which all are equally invited by God," in the words of Pope John Paul II. Can we see what a difference it makes when we define ourselves not as consumers and rivals but as grateful recipients of the gift of life, all invited to sit at the table? Hosts and guests.

Taking and Giving Communion

The great religious traditions teach that we find out who we are only in relationship with others. One twentieth-century mystic put it this way: "Insofar as I am not loved, I am unintelligible to myself." We can't make sense of our lives or of our world unless we know that we are noticed, valued, and cared for. Even when there is no human "other," a sense of connection with nature or an animal can make all the difference between happiness and misery in some lives. For the religious person, God or Spirit is that who loves us and cares for us.

We find the sacred meal in many traditions. Think of the central ritual of communion in Christian practice. One name for Holy Communion is Eucharist, which is simply the Greek word for "thanksgiving." The sacrament tells us that the world is a table with room for everyone and plenty of food for all our needs. It is a powerful social and political sign as well as a spiritual one. A friend writes, "I have come to a deeper understanding of what a severe form of punishment the practice of excommunicating (literally, severing the common connection by denying one partaking of Communion) individuals from the church was and is." It made the person's world unintelligible. We only make sense to ourselves in some kind of communion.

What was revolutionary about Jesus was his willingness to widen the circle of hospitality to include the world's outcasts. Nonbelievers and believers alike can appreciate the radical nature of inviting everyone to come to the table.

Native Americans celebrated their sense of solidarity with all creatures in honoring the animals they killed for sustenance: deer, buffalo, salmon, bear. It's only recently that we've lost touch with the idea of our food coming from our connections with all life. The idea is that other beings—plants and animals—sacrifice themselves for our well-being and deserve our thanks because we all participate in a dance of transformation. And maybe we are involved in this sacrifice, too.

The Dandelion Story

There's a story of a dandelion having a conversation with the nutrients in the earth. "Say, how would you like to become dandelion?" The nutrients were dubious. "What would that mean for us? How could that happen?" The dandelion told them that when the rain came they would dissolve in water and the plant would then draw them up by its roots. Whatever it took into its system would become "dandelion," and the dandelion would thus grow. The nutrients, after a lot of debate, agreed.

Later, a rabbit hopped up to the dandelion to ask if the plant were committed to transformation. "Say, dandelion, how would you like to become rabbit?" The dandelion wanted to run—the last thing it could do, of course. "What would be involved in my being transformed into 'rabbit'?" The rabbit confessed that the dandelion would have to consent to be torn to shreds and eaten, but the rabbit would flourish and the dandelion would be transformed. The plant agreed and rabbit ate it up and hopped along the path, only to run into a hunter—who in turn asked the rabbit the ominous question: "Say, rabbit, how would you like to become human?" The rabbit gulped and asked what would happen. "The deal is this. I kill you, skin you, and cook you in a pan over my campfire and then I eat you."

The rabbit, full of hope and fear, agrees. After a hearty lunch the hunter continues on his way. The story abruptly ends with the hunter hearing a voice above the trees, "Say, hunter, how would you like to become divine?"

We are all in this cycle of life and one day it will be our turn to let go and give up our lives. The way we do it will depend on how we have lived. Living gratefully in communion prepares us for the final letting go. Understanding that we are both host and guest on the planet gives us the dance steps to move through life generously and with grace.

❧

Gratitude Practice: A Place at the Table

1. Find a local soup kitchen and volunteer. Be a host to those who are hungry. See where this might lead.

2. "Before you taste anything, recite a blessing," said the Rabbi Akiva. Learn the habit of saying grace at your feasts. This is a practice open to all; you don't have to be formally religious or even think of yourself as religious. If you understand yourself to be on a spiritual path, then saying grace will come naturally. One ritual Alan has enjoyed at a friend's house (and this friend cannot stand organized religion) was simply sitting around the table holding hands, each telling the others why they were thankful. It's that simple. The great barrier is often our self-consciousness.

3. Invite someone you wouldn't ordinarily have thought of to dinner at your home. Ask a friend or family member to bring someone new. This needs careful handling and a dedication on your part to be open to the new, allow yourself to be surprised. Alan tended to be prejudiced about loud modern popular music until he had dinner with a rock musician, who introduced him to a new world of powerful rhythm and sound. He still doesn't like the music but has a new respect for those who do. The world is a larger and lovelier world because of that meal. So, think of a world that is terra incognita to you, find someone from that unknown land, and invite them to dinner. Simply pay attention to that person and learn.

4. Invite friends to dinner—preferably a potluck—and create a symposium. Agree with your guests in advance on a topic, perhaps involving some background reading, film viewing, or the like, and gently guide the conversation. Make sure everyone is heard from.

5. How good are you at receiving? When someone serves you in a store or restaurant, acknowledge their service with genuine thanks in addition to a tip, if appropriate.

6. Experiment with fasting. It can be done for different reasons: to cleanse the system, rid the body of persistent infections, or, of course, shed some pounds. But we suggest that a primary purpose might be to express solidarity with and share something of the experience of people who are hungry in the world. A sunset-to-sunset fast once or twice a week for a set period of time (Lent is a traditional one) can be good for body and soul without any risk of physical harm.

Imagine what the world could be like if we acted as host to everyone we met, and everyone we met treated us as an honored guest?

17

Grateful Connections

Gratefulness waters old friendships and makes new ones sprout.
—RUSSIAN PROVERB

John's consulting work with people in business centers on how relationships develop, change, and function (or don't) in the workplace. In this context he's observed a lot of relationships and heard even more relationship stories. Interestingly, personal "nonwork" relationships come up in conversations about workplace issues almost as frequently as stories about coworkers. Our careers and personal lives are not as separate as we might like to think. And he always spots a red flag when someone in business speaks and behaves in ways that make clear he or she has one standard for how to relate to people in personal life, but a different standard at work.

Forming and maintaining connections is the central task of our adult life, as any expert in psychology or spiritual development will confirm. To draw a parallel with the biochemical nervous system, these human-to-human connections are the pathways across which the life-sustaining elixir of gratitude travels back and forth. Forming a connection—sensing and responding to the attraction that draws us into relationship with others—stimulates our gratitude; and sustaining that connection over time depends on an ever-renewed supply of the wondrous substance.

In this chapter we'll explore how that dynamic works. Our main focus is on intimate partnerships, but we are convinced that it works in basically the same way regardless of whether our attachment is to a lover, a parent, a coworker, a beloved place or institution, an avocation, or a career.

The Urge to Connect

On a trip to New York following the horrific events of September 11, 2001, John found a palpable urge among New Yorkers to reconnect. Like countless others he was amazed to experience a sincere reaching out from cab drivers and clerks to strangers on the street. "It was as if an unknown force was emanating from the tower craters, drawing us together. We felt grateful for the simple presence of life going on around us, and for the smallest transaction that brought us into contact with each other."

On the other side of the continent, John heard the story of a loving attachment that bloomed between two veterans of serial unfulfilling relationships who found each other in their middle years. Sydney, a tough-minded community organizer, had slashed through myriad affairs and one short-lived marriage in her 41 years. She had given up trying to find a special other when she happened to meet Ian, a reserved, 43-year-old Scotsman who had recently migrated to her hometown of Seattle. Ian was a civil engineer who had moved around the construction world from project to project. Angular, shy, and self-sufficient, all six-foot-three of him seemed well armored against yet another relationship that would be truncated when he moved on.

They shared a love of nature, especially hiking, and first met in early December on a hike in the woods of the Olympic Peninsula. Both long of leg and fit, they soon found themselves far ahead of the others, exchanging polite trail talk. Both assumed the acquaintance would end there, but a month later they discovered they had again signed up for the same hike. Again they found themselves striding well ahead. Only this time a small crisis intervened when Ian twisted his ankle badly on a wet, moss-covered rock.

Sydney remembers,

> When Ian went down, all 220 pounds of him, I knew it was up to me to look after him. His ankle was swelling fast and he was in serious

pain. Luckily there was a road fairly near, and I could support him getting that far. We flagged a ride to an emergency room.

From that time on our attachment has grown. He needed help, asked for it, and was quick to express his gratitude for it. I was happy to help and had no expectations in giving it. That simple give-and-take experience, as basic as it seems, was vital for us, kind of a kick start that brought us outside ourselves and made us really start to see each other. What we found were two fairly like-minded, independent people . . . probably the only kind of person either of us could build a strong relationship with. But we also found that we weren't as self-sufficient as we had believed.

We'll revisit Sydney and Ian's story for insights about the nature of particular attachments. One important quality of such relationships is that they be based in the specific and real. In Chapter 2 we lamented a trend toward what we called "virtual" living, aided by a comment from the literary critic Roger Scruton. When we opt to inhabit some mass-produced version of reality, says Scruton, "Any part can be replaced by an equivalent which will 'do just as well,' and the attachment of people who are attached to particulars—to wives, and lovers, to projects and ambitions, to sacred places and 'imagined communities'—begins to seem faintly comic. . . ."

It is the "particulars" of life that give it shape, richness, and distinctive flavors, and the particularity of our relationships that makes them strong, sustaining, and resilient. We think of particular attachments as wearing well, growing in power and significance over time. They cannot easily be replaced by an equivalent that will "do just as well." The healthiest connections are founded and fueled on gratitude, as we shall see.

What Makes an Attachment Grateful?

Grateful connections are a gift of maturity. Children, of course, form very strong and deep attachments, but because they're still basically in the self-referencing stage of development, their attachments are different in nature from the relationships of psychological adulthood. It's not within the scope of this book to detail what so many relationship manuals have spent hundreds of pages on, but we'll try to summarize our sense of the qualities that characterize positive attachments, then look more closely at how the gratitude dynamic operates around them.

- Noticing the unique qualities of the other
- Desire to know the other, and to be known
- Empathy and imagination
- Trust based on authenticity and truthfulness
- A sense of fairness and balance
- Accepting responsibility and obligation
- Flexibility, adaptability, patience, and humor
- Shared values, goals, and projects
- Compassion and forgiveness

This is a fair-sized laundry list for mature adult relationships, and each item has been dissected thoroughly by writers more expert than us. What we want to do here is examine how gratitude serves to bring forth these qualities in particular attachments. How does practicing gratitude feed and replenish the right stuff of relationships? We can see this as a kind of parallel journey to developing our individual gratitude practice. It begins in like fashion with simple noticing and grows through various stages, until the gifts of a sound relationship ultimately feed back into and nourish the greater world.

Sydney and Ian had spent years seeking connection with others in barren places. Earlier failures had left them swathed in protective cynicism. But they found that under certain circumstances (a sprained ankle on a trail), the wonder of the other can strike forcefully enough to cut through the protective layers. They believe it started with Ian's expression of gratitude for Sydney's help. And we believe that all the most powerful connections—to a beloved, to God, or to a waif on the street, begin with a spark of gratitude. Let's look at where those sparks fly.

1. NOTICE AND KNOW THE OTHER

As in learning to cultivate gratitude for all of life's gifts, the first step in building a solid attachment is turning our focus outward, giving the other our attention. We can make no greater gift than to desire to know another deeply; we can receive no greater gift than to be entrusted with another's unguarded soul. Being moved to do either of those things requires, first, that fundamental mysterious attraction to the other (again, this may be a creature, a special place, or an endeavor as well as an adult human).

Then, to firm up and deepen the attachment calls for the conscious bestowing of attention, time after time. A readiness to gain understanding by eliciting the other's history, ideas, and fears; an ability to empathize with that one's experience and feelings; a sense of pleasure and reward in sharing the secrets of another self. It is this awareness of reward and gift from the attachment that gets gratitude flowing and keeps it flowing both ways. When we can recognize how much our own lives are enriched by what we discover in others, we are encouraged to seek greater intimacy. Unless the other is too deeply damaged and defended against being known, he or she likewise will be encouraged to give and accept this kind of attention.

2. Appreciate the Complexity of the Other

We might call this the "summer" phase of growing a particular attachment. Once we have begun to notice what attracts us in another, and to value what is different from ourselves, we have the chance to explore further—as deeply as we wish and the other will permit. Discovering a human being in all of his or her complexity is one of life's great adventures, and over time, if both parties continue to grow, there will always be more to discover.

3. Show Generosity to the Other

As attachments mature, they are invariably tested: by conflicting desires and priorities; by the stresses of work, money, or child rearing; by the pull of other attachments; and by sheer, stubborn self-interest—something no one ever grows out of completely. In the "autumn" of our relationships we need more than ever to extend generosity toward the other, to cultivate the qualities of fairness, trust, mutual acceptance of responsibility, flexibility, patience, and forgiveness.

If there is a firm foundation of gratitude for the gifts the other brings to the relationship, and for the relationship itself, these essential qualities are likely to spring forth when needed.

Let's look briefly at how gratitude might operate in a different kind of a relationship: a business partnership. Partnerships of all kinds contain the potential to foster healthy special attachments, but few reach that potential. Recent studies show that more than seventy percent of business alliances fail to reach the goals they originally set. In business—as well as in personal relationships—there are three main sources for that failure:

- The parties fail to agree on what they expect from each other in specific terms, and on how inequities are to be quickly remedied.
- The rules of engagement are seldom clear; indeed, they are often purposely obfuscated to give one party an edge. When power struggles ensue, rules are neglected or changed capriciously, rendering them useless.
- There are usually no rituals for partners to express their gratitude for the rich contributions of the other(s).

One business partnership John knows well has survived robustly for more than thirty-five years with one partner in New York and the other in San Francisco. When pressed for the reasons for their unusual success, the partners offered the following summary: "We both work hard at our tasks. We have a clear understanding about our roles and objectives, we live by our rules, and we talk almost every day. And we like each other!" When asked how they dealt with disagreements, one answered, "We have rules for that too and we stick with them: for example, settle differences quickly and firmly and don't go over old stuff." John notes that they also celebrate with each other on a regular basis.

4. GIVE BACK FROM THE RELATIONSHIP

The fruits of a rich, mature, particular attachment are not enjoyed solely by the primary parties in it. In this Winter section of the book, we talk about how a life of practicing gratitude is one lived in community. Great marriages, great friendships, passions faithfully followed, a lifelong devotion to one's art: all these are particular attachments that give something back to the world. Shared values, goals, and projects may move to the heart of a relationship as it matures; they can even survive the physical death of one of the partners.

There are many ways in which successful life partnerships give back to their communities. Such couples can set a much-needed example in an age when commitments seem so seldom to endure. Not by putting up a false front but by sharing their struggles, crises and triumphs with others close to them. Strong couples with children, of course, give the great gift of raising loving, responsible, productive human beings. Marriages in which one partner helps lead a spiritual community typically mean that both partners help lead.

Shared values and passions are important nutrients in life partnerships. Too many attachments come under stress not because beliefs are incompatible, but because the partners have no passionate beliefs at all. Being unable to share and exercise passion can throw people into peril: the tedium of daily strains goes unrelieved, the need for external stimulation and entertainment increases, and insidious games can replace purposeful activity—withholding feelings or demanding more feelings than the partner has in his or her emotional bank.

In David McCullough's biography of John Adams, he pays considerable attention to the bonds of love and shared values that connected John and Abigail Adams so strongly to each other and to their extended family and community. Their frequent letters express immense gratitude and admiration for each other and for their opportunities to serve an emerging nation.

One of the most positive people we know is a widow now in her sixties, who with her husband built a wonderful marriage but has had hard times since he died much too early. Bright but with no employable skills, Mildred had to work menial jobs to support their three young children, while going back to school. But she not only endured, she prevailed.

Bill and Mildred during their marriage grew deep connections with other family, friends, and community, which now sustain Mildred—and vice versa. She is indefatigable and remarkably generous with her time but quick to point out how grateful she is for opportunities to serve. "Through volunteering and being available for friends and family in need, I get enormous satisfaction. And I have met the most remarkable people who really enrich my life." Another hint about what leads her to give back: "I still remember those who reached out to me when my husband died. They kept me going until I could get my feet under me."

A gift for forming grateful connections is not limited to marriage. For thirty-five years Mildred and her brother have exchanged daily phone calls. "Mostly we just chat, but it always starts my day well to connect with my brother or my kids. Sometimes we really need each other, and by keeping in close track of what's going on, we can help before needs get out of hand."

Faith communities are often the first place where couples reach out to help and be helped—though it can be challenging in these times of great career mobility. A couple in their early forties told Alan that one reason their marriage had survived seven moves in nine years was their ability to connect with a new community quickly. "We get actively involved in the kids' school and a church as soon as possible. We shop the local churches of our denomination until we find the right one. Through volunteering we meet people, and it helps us get past the strangeness of yet another new house and neighborhood."

It is through our most particular attachments that we're compelled to give the most, risk the most, and stand to learn the most about gratitude.

Gratitude Practice: Growing Relationships

1. The weekly walk. Get outdoors with a loved one for a minimum half hour's walk at least once a week. Striding or strolling calms the spirit and loosens the tongue. Sharing a connection with nature (or the urban scene for that matter) can put your own issues in perspective. We know one busy couple in publishing that makes a point of meeting up for an early evening walk with their dog every day. "We trade tales of our very different days, bring a notepad to jot down those important dates we'd forgotten to tell each other about earlier, and check the pulse of our neighborhood."

2. The annual review. One forty-plus couple we know, a banker and a consultant, sit down at the start of each year and review "where the pinches are." They try to listen empathetically, acknowledge slights and jealousies, formally offer gratitude for

the other's support, and discuss what each needs to grow. They air dreams and hopes, and ask for support for the coming year. They feel it has helped their marriage work mostly very well for thirteen years, during good times and bad. The key: "We want the best for each other and we have developed trust. We don't judge the other's plans and needs."

3. The annual letter. This is a good practice for loved ones who don't live near each other. A friend says: "Each year I celebrate those I love by writing them a letter of thanks for our connection. I try to be very direct in expressing my love and respect and my hopes for our continuing connection. The letters range in length, but the core message is my appreciation for them and for our relationship."

18

Repairing the World

One can never pay in gratitude. One can only "pay in kind"
somewhere else in life.
                                    —ANNE MORROW LINDBERGH

You must be the change if you wish to change the world.
                                    —MAHATMA GANDHI

In the movie of J. R. R. Tolkein's classic *The Lord of the Rings,* the
Hobbit hero, Frodo, says, "I wish the ring had never come to me . . .
I wish none of this had happened." His mentor and friend, the wizard
Gandalf, replies, "So do all who live to see such times, but that is not
for them to decide. All we have to decide is what to do with the time
that is given us."

Gandalf's wise response reveals the key to the spiritual life, which
is will or choice. We cannot decide when to live our lives but we can
decide how. People have always been drawn to myths and stories that
help them understand why they feel trapped by circumstances and yet
free to act at the same time. We feel powerless yet also part of something bigger than ourselves, through which we may be able to act
effectively. We are connected (or sense that we once were) to a larger
and more generous world.

One of Rilke's poems talks about "the law of the stars" that is written in our hearts. He describes our ache for deep connection in a cry

for solidarity with the universe: "Ah, not to be cut off, / not through the slightest partition / shut out from the law of the stars. / The inner— what is it? / if not intensified sky, / hurled through with birds and deep / with the winds of homecoming."

Myths of various traditions suggest that human origins are divine (something like Rilke's "intensified sky"). Most try to explain how we got here and to answer two impossible questions: How did the world come to be such a wonderful place? And why is it in such a mess? In the biblical tale of the Garden of Eden with its Tree of the Knowledge of Good and Evil, Adam and Eve couldn't handle this knowledge and were banished from the Garden. Thus their descendants experience the prison of time and circumstance, and yet remain free to respond to the times.

If the world is so great, why does it need fixing? That's the eternal, probably unanswerable, question, and we are left to figure out how to live with it. People in every age have to find ways to be grateful for the world as it is, and ways of repairing the world. Our choices matter.

Mending Creation

One of our favorite origin stories comes from the Jewish mystical tradition, the Kabbalah. This wonderful story tries to explain the glory and brokenness of the world and the important role humans can play in repairing what has been broken. This is Alan's retelling:

> In the beginning before there were any beginnings and endings, there was no place that was not already God! And we call this unimaginable openness Ain Soph: Being without end. Then came the urge to give life to our world and to us. But there was no place that was not already God. So Ain Soph breathed in to make room, like a father steps back so his child will walk to him. Into the emptiness Ain Soph set vessels and began to fill them with divine light, as a mother places bowls in which to pour her delicious soup. As the light poured forth a perfect world was being created!
>
> Think of it! A world without greed and cruelty and violence! But then, something happened. The bowls shattered. No one knows

why. Perhaps the bowls were too frail? Perhaps the light too intense? Perhaps Ain Soph was learning. After all no one makes perfect the first time. And with the shattering of the bowls, divine sparks threw everywhere! Some rushing back to Ain Soph, some falling, falling, trapped in the broken shards to become our world, and us.

Though this is hard to believe, the perfect world is all around us, but broken into jagged pieces, like a puzzle thrown to the floor, the picture lost, each piece without meaning, until someone puts them back together again. We are that someone. There is no one else. We are the ones who can find the broken pieces, remember how they fit together and rejoin them. This is the repairing of the world— the mending of creation. In every moment, with every act, we can heal our world and us. We are all holy sparks dulled by separation.

But when we meet, and talk and eat and make love, when we work and play and disagree with holiness in our eyes, seeing Ain Soph everywhere, then our brokenness will end, and our bowls will be strong enough to hold the light, and our light will be gentle enough to fill the bowls. As we repair the world together, we will learn that there is no place that is not God!

We love many things about this story: its sense of vastness and wonder; the very human images of a father stepping back to encourage his child to walk to him and a mother making her delicious soup. The idea that we each have important work to do, and that it's done in the dailiness of life. The possibility of joining together to repair a broken world.

When we are awake we can see the movement from astonishment to gratitude, and from gratitude to service. We're able to see life as a cycle of blessing—being blessed and blessing in return. When we cultivate a grateful response to existence, there arises an inevitable urge to give back, to repair what has been broken. The world is, by definition, that which I share with all things. The German word is *Mitwelt,* the "world-with."

The challenge is in seeing that everything is connected. And the discipline of learning *how* this works—in fine detail, ecologically, socially, and spiritually—may be our most important task in the current millennium. We are learning more and more about deep systems in science and economics. Everything is either a system or a component of a system. There is no isolated object. The catch is: this concept is easy to articulate but exceedingly hard to internalize and act upon.

Solidarity with All

A friend of Alan's defines spirituality as "the art of making connections." Alan was reminded of this while watching a documentary about clearcutting in forests of the Northwest. "What went through my mind as I saw the bald hills denuded of their trees was another TV image, the one of East Los Angeles after the beating of Rodney King."

Both were pictures of war zones on a wounded planet. East L.A. and the ravaged forest are connected in being the objects of abuse or neglect. The horrors of racial hatred and polluting pristine rivers, indifference to the poor and the squandering of natural resources, are linked. Ecology is a prism through which we can see and celebrate the sacred community of all life. It should be something about which to rejoice. Once we see that, we become environmentalists in the broadest sense.

Buddhist teachings explicitly aim for the complete identification of the individual spirit with the universe, and acknowledge how elusive that goal is. A Buddhist tale from medieval Vietnam portrays this knowledge as a secret guarded in a deep cave:

A monk asked Chân Không, "What is the wondrous Dharma?"

Chân Không said, "You will know only after you have awakened."

The monk said, "I have not been able to understand your previous instructions, so how can I understand your present teaching?"

Chân Không said, "If you go to the deep caves where the immortals dwell, you will be able to bring back the elixir that will transform you."

The monk asked, "What is the elixir?"

Chân Không said, "Through eons of ignorance, you do not comprehend it, but the morning of enlightenment you open up into illumination."

The monk asked, "What is illumination?"

Chân Không said, "Illumination shines through the whole world [revealing that] all sentient beings are together in a single family."

The theme of solidarity with all beings is echoed by South Africa's Archbishop Desmond Tutu, responding to the question, "Will there be people in Heaven?" "Oh, yes!" he replied, "Heaven is community. A solitary human being is a contradiction. In Africa we say that a person is a person through other persons."

The grateful response of desiring to repair the world is reinforced every time we catch a glimpse of our connection to the web of life. The old maxim is "the pattern that connects is the pattern that corrects." True perceptions of solidarity breed gratitude, compassion, and the need to act.

We've seen that spirit of grateful connecting come vividly alive in friends who have helped others rebuild their lives after an accident or an illness. Something happens, and we are brought up short by our common vulnerability. We find that we need others, even if only for the simple reason that we cannot see clearly on our own. We need the perspective of others because our worldview is often damaged and distorted. It's not only the world that needs repairing. We do too. It's easy to confuse our personal version of events with objective truth.

A prison volunteer named Joe, who reached adulthood with a fairly firm sense of having most of the answers, came to recognize through his volunteering experience that his worldview was in need of expanding:

A friend talked me into volunteering at a nearby county jail, doing weekly Bible studies with the inmates. I couldn't have felt less qualified on any front to present myself as an authority to these men. My parents were well-to-do, and I was raised in a loving and whole family. I had no teaching background, and though we were closely involved in the Episcopal church, I had no prior experience studying the Bible. And of course I'd led a pretty sheltered life: a great education, no criminal background, no poverty or substance abuse.

I had no real-world experience or qualifications to be inside a jail, yet I was welcomed, taken seriously, depended on to show up every week, and appreciated. I always left the jail feeling grateful for the opportunity and experience of being "inside" one more time, and never felt that I had given more than I had received for the few hours I'd been there. I was grateful to the men who welcomed me into their community and appreciated whatever I had to offer—they taught me a lot about prayer, spirituality, and the importance of

Scripture. And I keep "getting back" from that experience. I've had ex-inmates come up to me unexpectedly on the street, months or years later, and thank me for having helped them.

The Gap Between Knowing and Practicing

Sometimes, even with a well-developed sense of gratitude and high idealism about wanting to repair the world, we find ourselves frozen in inaction, not knowing where or how to start. Like the eleventh-century yogi Naropa, who knew the theory of compassion backwards and forwards yet could not bear to look at a lice-infested dog, we can be crippled by idealism and feel like hypocrites for not practicing what we believe.

We could use some compassion for ourselves at this point. Those attuned to suffering may often feel overwhelmed by the world's pain, depressed to the point of hopelessness. Or simply fearful of what we will encounter by extending a hand, putting ourselves in contact with those whose lives are so much more broken than our own.

There are ways to get past these barriers of fear and hopelessness, and beating ourselves up because we can't do more is not productive. Acknowledging the limits of our courage and capacity to risk keeps us open to grace. And it's not always bad to feel caught between a rock and a hard place. As Buddhist teacher Pema Chodron comments,

> With both the upliftedness of our ideas and the rawness of what is happening in front of our eyes—that is indeed a very fruitful place. When we feel squeezed, there's a tendency for the mind to become small. We feel miserable, like a victim, like a pathetic, hopeless case. So believe it or not, at that moment of hassle or bewilderment or embarrassment, our minds could become bigger. . . . The next time there's no ground to stand on, don't consider it an obstacle. Consider it a remarkable stroke of luck. We have no ground to stand on, and at the same time it could soften and inspire us. Finally, after all these years, we could truly grow up.

Indeed, for some people the challenge is not to rush ahead putting our convictions into practice when we don't know the territory. History is replete with examples of well-intentioned interventions that turned out disastrously. The attempts of Western nations to develop poor agricultural countries are a whole category of such misguided "repair" jobs. One could think of the noble experiment of communism in a similar way.

We all know what a pain do-gooders can be. "Hello! I've come to repair the world, and your world in particular. Stand aside!" Zealotry is as dangerous as indifference. C. S. Lewis commented that there are a lot of people going around "doing good," and you can tell the people being done good to by the hunted expression in their eyes! And W. H. Auden impishly remarked something like: "We were put on earth to help others. What the others are supposed to do I haven't a clue!"

The Power of Something Larger

We do not have to be on top, in control, or in the driver's seat to feel we are participating, paid-up members of the world community. We can join the soul "in its textured and maddening entanglement with everything that comes its way," as David Whyte puts it. What works for many people, as a way to take part in repairing creation, is to allow oneself to become part of a larger endeavor. It works for both those who wish to be helpers and those in need of help (we are all both at one time or another).

Alan tells the story of Roger, a homeless man who slept most nights in a portal of the cathedral where Alan works. Roger seemed a hopeless case; in fact, one of Alan's colleagues said, "Oh! He's beyond repair." He was offered a place in a local homeless shelters but said he didn't feel safe there. Cathedral personnel decided to let Roger be for a while.

One day a grubby envelope arrived in Alan's internal mail. Inside was a beautiful meticulous drawing of the old cathedral house, and a note: "I thought you might like this. My name's Roger. I'm the homeless person sleeping in the North Portal."

To make a long story short, Alan found some money to buy Roger art supplies and also put him in touch with the Veterans Benefits Administration. It turned out he qualified for disability, and he is now a full-time artist with his own web site. The point is that Roger made a choice to reach out with his art. It was a small move, just his way of thanking those who let him be. Others made choices to respond. Later Roger expressed his thanks for (he said) getting his life back by presenting the cathedral with an enlarged full-color copy of the same lovely drawing.

Alan once asked Roger what had kept him going. "I held on to my art," he said, "because it connects me with something larger than myself. All I needed were pencils and paper to be transported to a world where I wasn't just a homeless guy looking for a meal and shower. I was part of something bigger. And when I sent that picture to you, I knew I was part of a community."

Sometimes we are overtaken unexpectedly by a chance to make a difference in the world. A friend of John's, a meditation scholar named Paul, heard about a woman who was dying and whose chief wish was to have a conversation with a famous teacher of contemplative prayer. She didn't know how to go about initiating such a contact, but Paul knew the teacher and was able to bring them together. He felt a euphoria after this had happened, he says, "as if I had just stepped into some powerful tide of 'what was supposed to happen' and helped it along."

The Elements of Building Community

What does it take to "repair the world"? The late John W. Gardner, social philosopher and adviser to presidents, outlined what he believed were the elements of a good community, one concerned with individual integrity and respect for differences. High value is given to cooperation, to mutual need, and to acknowledging the hard work and accomplishments of others. All these, he admits, sound like the values of compassion and altruism found in the great religions. In a good community, he writes, there is "a sense of belonging and identity, a spirit of mutual responsibility. . . . There is trust and tolerance and loyalty. Everyone is included. There is room for mavericks, nonconformists and dissenters. There are no outcasts." Everyone has a place at the table.

Love is at the heart of repairing the world. Why? Because love is the greatest act of the imagination; only through love can we imagine a community of radically differing individuals. Love also accepts the transitoriness of our social arrangements and institutions. Anyone who has tried to love completely knows what a mess we make of it. That's why the world needs repairing and why we need to build forgiveness into all our relationships.

The Force of Joy

The "ideal" community is about celebration too. Don't we want to live in a world where we don't need an excuse to throw a party and invite the neighbors? Communities need to discover reasons to celebrate sheer human courage and tenacity; celebrate how people do what they must do, day in and day out. The single mother getting the kids off to school, worrying how they will fare from three to six while she's still at work, hoping the neighbor will keep faith and keep then safe. The old man living alone, wondering how he'll make it through the day. The pressured leader wondering if he can take the heat one more day. People are weak and pathetic but they are also brave and wonderful, going on in their muddle, pain, and exhaustion. There are reasons to celebrate.

In parts of Africa it's said that there are those who are born to die (or even to be killed), those who are born to survive, and those who are born to live. In places where violence, sickness, and mortality are high, the survivors have a constant awareness of life as a gift—more than most of us who enjoy good health and extended lifetimes. Examples abound of fortunate individuals from poor societies who get an education abroad and return home to dedicate themselves—as doctors, engineers, agricultural experts, or the like—to giving back.

We are the blessed. How do we respond? One small step to building the temple of reconciliation is the effort to simplify our lives in solidarity with most of the rest of the world.

Called to Be Subversives

Building a society that is open and flexible rather than repressive requires individual members who are willing to be subversive. Willing to be subversive means having our eyes opened to what's going on in our neighborhood, and changing the rules if they need changing. The character of Coyote the Trickster in Native American myth is always turning the established order upside-down for creative ends.

Through subversive acts, grateful repairers can help marginalized outsiders break the boundaries that keep them out. The community we build together has to be both sustaining and subversive, both maintaining and disturbing the social order.

We're reminded of a statement in Wendell Berry's short story "The Wild Birds." The character Burley Coulter says, "The way we are, we are members of each other. All of us. Everything. The difference ain't in who is a member and who is not, but in who knows and who don't."

The Third Place

Roy Oldenburg, author of *The Great Good Place,* writes that a healthy and balanced social identity has historically relied on three factors: family, work, and "a third place." This third place provides people with new stimulation, fresh perspectives on life, a spiritual dimension, and an open and inclusive society. Its essential requirements are that:

1. It is neutral ground
2. Rank is forgotten
3. Conversation is the central activity
4. It is frequented by a core group of regulars
5. It fosters playful interpersonal exchange

In England the third place has traditionally been the pub; in France, the sidewalk cafe and bistro; the coffee bar in Italy; the biergarten in Germany; and the after-hours private clubs in Japan. Another place that once served these functions was the church. In times past, the church wasn't just for narrowly "religious" purposes. It was a place where the community met, not just for public worship, celebration, or mourning but for social occasions as well. In the United States today it's hard to think of many places that fulfill these needs. (The nostalgic appeal of the TV show *Cheers* surely is based on our need for a third place.)

Oldenburg concludes, "Without the Third Place, a society fails to nourish the kinds of relationships and diversity of human contact that are essential to a psychologically balanced life."

One of the tasks of building community is to nurture mutual trust and a sense of ease among its members. The third place is a valuable venue for doing this: intrinsically democratic, nonhierarchical, its main purpose one of social interaction. Out of such fellowship, social entities often engage in communal tasks: scholarship funds, building efforts, sponsoring kids' teams, aid to those in need. Groups like the Elks and the Rotary, certainly churches, and even some commercial establishments have supported such community projects.

But those older institutions are in danger of vanishing, and we need creative thinking about what will replace them. The workplace is sometimes a venue for giving back, but lacks the true social qualities of a third place. Various constituencies of a community have their organizations—health-based support groups, land-protection groups, and so on—but as leisure time has eroded, so have the occasions for people to gather in neighborhood or village social life. We'd do well to attend to this foundational need of building community.

It Starts with You

> Independence? That's a middle-class blasphemy. We are all
> dependent on one another, every soul of us on earth.
> —GEORGE BERNARD SHAW

John Gardner suggests the following tests for any effort to begin building community. Determine who are the most influential citizens at every level of your city or town—in the neighborhoods, in civic organizations, corporations, unions, churches, minority groups, the professions, and so on. Then ask yourself these questions: Do they know one another? Have they ever met to discuss the future of their shared place? Have they made real efforts to understand one another, to work together?

For most cities the answer will be no. So what do you do? You could start by making a telephone call related to your chief passion: something life has given you and that you want others to share. When action springs from gratitude rather than abstract zeal or anger, something capable of mending creation is born.

A political and social vision that starts with personal commitment can build a more just society. So ask yourself some questions, too: Are you a scapegoater or a forgiver? Do you romanticize violence or do you repudiate it? Do you give others a chance to show how they are lovable? Or how they might love you?

We all have a right to be cherished. This is not the same as saying we have the right to be spoiled rotten. The right to be adored has to do with our intrinsic dignity as persons and the sheer delight of our uniqueness. Maybe the best place to begin repairing the world is to ask whom do you need to forgive—beginning with yourself. Who needs to forgive you? Giving and receiving forgiveness is one of the primary skills of a grateful heart. It is part of the craft. Forgiving and cherishing each other are first steps toward repairing the world.

Gratitude Practice: Repairing the World

In addition to thinking about these issues for yourself, trying talking them over with someone you know and trust—as well as with someone you don't know well. Give each other equal time in the conversation.

1. Describe an experience you've had of effective cooperation. What was the project? What are the values and lessons you draw from that experience? What are the gifts and talents you brought to the table?
2. Imagine you are speaking to a group of children about what is most important in life, what really matters. What would you say?

3. How do you imagine a better world? What does the world you want to live in look like? Be specific. Then imagine that the world you live in thirty years from now is similar to your vision of a better world. What did you do to make it happen?

4. Do you have a Third Place? If so, what and where is it?

We begin to mend the world when a grateful heart reaches out to others. Let's look each other in the eye and argue and laugh the world back together.

19

Mortal Gratitude

Whoever has lived long enough to find out what life is, knows how deep a debt of gratitude we owe to Adam, the first great benefactor of our race. He brought death into the world.

—MARK TWAIN

Remember the 1998 film, *As Good as It Gets,* with fine performances by Jack Nicholson, Helen Hunt, and Greg Kinnear? Many of us loved it because it managed to be funny and heartrending at the same time, a lot like life. And its ambiguous title sums up the existential questions we're always asking life: *Is* this as good as it gets? And is what we get *good*?

In what way is life good? How can it be good if it is regularly punctuated with heartbreak and ends in obliteration? These are the tough questions humans have asked since consciousness arose: the basis and ultimate challenge of all faiths. There are no easy answers, but there are ways to live with the question. The secret lies in the choices we make during life's winter—and we use "winter" both chronologically and experientially.

When the frost of winter hardens our experience of the world, we have choices. We can simply endure. We can fight it and make it worse. We can wait in hope, knowing that even winter doesn't last forever.

Moving Through the Seasons

We're nearing the end of our journey through the seasons. We've seen that gratitude is a lifelong practice that starts with being open to the unexpected. We've thought about our response to creation and our unique place in it, about the soul-opening gifts of nature and the complicated legacy of family. We've sought ways to be grateful even for painful experiences and relationships; enjoyed the blessings of the body and play; acknowledged our debt to the arts and the life of the mind.

We know to honor our need for rest and down time. We've explored the thickets of morality and the search for integrity in our work and personal lives. We have come to appreciate that we are actors in an inherited drama that echoes through history. We have considered the spiritual basis of gratitude. We've learned the joy of giving back to the community something of what we've been given.

The more we describe the lineaments of gratitude in all its forms, the closer we get to our own fragility and vulnerability. This life doesn't last for ever, and time is running out. Winter is upon us.

What Do We Mean by Good?

Scotty McLennan, in *Finding Your Religion*, quotes a woman who had some negative experiences with the religion of her childhood and who as an adult began to discover *goodness* in a new way. "I began to see not only that my being good wasn't God's chief concern, but that, in an entirely different way, *God* was good," she says. "Not good as in 'behave yourself,' but *good*. Like pizza and beer for dinner when you're tired and hungry. Like a hot bath, or a great day, or holding your kids: that kind of good. I wanted more of Him."

This speaks of our longing to be "good" in the sense that a tree or a flower is good. They are good and sufficient and whole simply by *being*. Goodness—the longing for life in its fullness—is like what? You fill in the blanks.

It's not a matter of being religious or not. It's a tricky matter of seeing the goodness in ordinary things. A tree is "good" because it doesn't have an identity crisis! It just gets on with being itself. Your dog or cat has a way of being in the world that we might call "good." Sophie,

Alan's dog, is a companionable presence simply in herself. We tend to think of ourselves as above trees or dogs or cats, yet find it hard to be grateful for just getting up in the morning. We aim for grand gestures, when all we have to do is acknowledge the bliss of a slice of pizza or the glory of a hot bath.

Mortality: The Last Dragon

Underlying our ability to gratefully experience ordinary life is the wintry awareness that we're just passing through. We have had the privilege of meeting people compelled by myriad different circumstance to confront mortality, and who have found their way to gratitude in those struggles.

"Mortality" need not always mean death—it encompasses life's other profound pains and blows. When Alan heard that he'd been diagnosed with prostate cancer, he felt as if the bottom had fallen out of his world. To hear him talk now, you'd think it was the best thing that ever happened to him. Well, not quite. But he knows he's not under a death sentence and that thousands of men his age have the same kind of disease. He also enjoys the deep irony that it took getting cancer for him to take his health seriously.

> I've never felt better. And the regime I'm on has changed how I think and feel about life. I've talked about the diet and exercise, and the techniques to reduce stress have paid off in untold ways. Things that used to matter don't any more. And for the first time there's a kind of harmony between "me" and all the bits and pieces that I am. It's hard to describe; words like peace, integrity, acceptance and joy come to mind. I know I'm not immortal, but being aware of that now in my blood and bones makes me feel more alive.

When we talked about dragons in Chapter 7, we identified death as the biggest of them. Along with a couple of others, time and love, it is one of the great uncontrollables. Love cannot be forced, bought, or commanded. Time cannot be stopped. Most of the time we think we've just got to endure it, get through it. We can even be optimistic: "There's plenty of time," we say. "Time heals all wounds." But it doesn't. We tell ourselves, like a character in Michael Cunningham's novel *The Hours,* "But there are still the hours, aren't there? One and then another, and you get through that one and then, my god, there's another."

And what has all this waiting been in aid of? Ultimately, death. Death is inevitable. Facing our death and dying has to be part of our long-term strategy, if don't want that dragon to scare us into a living grave.

Paying Life's Price

We all know we are going to die one day, but we typically don't take this dragon really seriously until something comes along to knock us over the head. We lose our job, we have an accident, we get sick, we lose a loved one or a marriage—life falls apart. The great religions teach us that a lively sense of mortality can be the doorway to intense participation in life.

But it can also be a terror that closes us off to living fully. For some this blow can come early. Belden C. Lane writes, in *The Solace of Fierce Landscapes,*

> The first death I faced was my father's, which came with sudden, frightening violence then I was thirteen years old [from suicide or murder. It was never resolved]. At that time the dread beast, its wings flapping and breath as foul as hell, took by two shots in the chest the one I'd loved and feared most in all the world. This death had been the monster of chaos, intruding into life in a dramatic way. It left me locked in combat, teaching me to expect tragedy, prepare for sudden loss, and endure pain by making myself numb.
>
> In the gradual dying of my mother, however, death was very different. It came slowly as a teacher and as distant friend, offering passage through the wide, gray terrain of the mundane. It didn't threaten so much as it tired.

Our common struggle with death in the abstract becomes a life-and-death matter when the reality strikes close to home.

Life leaves its marks, and they won't be cosmetically concealed by enforced cheer or false optimism. Alan has a dread that when he's dying, people will come and see him and try to cheer him up. In his own work with the dying, he knows that the best friend is the one who is simply present and refuses to fill up the silences—no matter how awkward—with clichés about things being fine. Few things are worse than someone telling us "things will be all right" when they're not.

Comfort is possible, but it's always hard won. Jeannette Winterson, in her novel *Written on the Body,* writes:

> "You'll get over it . . ." It's the clichés that cause the trouble. To lose someone you love is to alter your life forever. You don't get over it because "It" is the person you loved. The pain stops, there are new people, but the gap never closes. How could it? . . . The fluttering in the stomach goes away and the full waking pain. Sometimes I think of you and feel giddy. Memory makes me lightheaded, drunk on champagne. All the things we did. And if anyone has said this was the price, I would have agreed to pay it. That surprises me; that with the hurt and the mess comes a shaft of recognition. It was worth it. Love is worth it.

That last sentence is the big clue. Loving makes it worth it. Love is as good as it gets. Out of the soul's experience of life in all its wintry chill, its raw meaninglessness, comes a ray of hope. Love doesn't make it "all right," but it does make it worth it.

All Kinds of Deaths

On some primal level, we know that we must simply live on in the face of death. If we forget this, we can be rendered catatonic. In Samuel Beckett's play, *Waiting for Godot,* one character says to the other, "Well, shall we go?" The other replies, "Yes, let's go." The stage directions after that state: *They do not move.* "This profound myth," observes Rollo May, "shows the depth of our human uncertainty." When we are in the middle of winter, life can move with painful slowness or even seem to cease moving. We can't go on. Yet we go on.

And while going on, we can notice things. We can pay attention. The character Vladimir cries to the boy, regarding Godot: "Tell him . . .

that you saw me." We long to be seen, to be noticed before we move on into we know not what. This is something we can do for each other.

Observing life's tragedies at a distance, as on stage, is one thing. We feel a chill, but we're not really challenged to wonder if we can go on. But sooner or later mortality will stand in our path. The worst, or what seems like it, will happen—for example, a parent faced with the death of a child.

When Sarah and Tony were called to the scene of a car accident a couple of miles from their house in rural Connecticut, they found their nine-year-old son, Danny, a mangled mess on the road. A neighbor had seen it happen and rushed to fetch them; they arrived just before the ambulance. They didn't know at first whether Danny was alive or dead. There was a great gash in his head; his jaw was twisted and his legs hung limp like a Raggedy Andy doll.

Danny lived, but for ten days Sarah and Tony didn't know whether he was permanently brain damaged. Strung up in a sling in the hospital, he stared and rolled his eyes in unrecognizing panic. On the tenth day, he looked at them and smiled—a twisted smile because of his broken jaw. But it was the best smile in the world: both Sarah and Tony burst into tears and were able to eat their first meal since the accident. There followed five weeks of daily visits to the hospital, nearly an hour away. A couple of weeks into this routine, Sarah turned to Tony and said, "I can't do this!" Then she laughed at herself and said, "I can do this!"

There are dramatic near-deaths and small, everyday deaths. Clarissa, a character in *The Hours,* ponders the feeling of being passed over by life. There's an image of life as a child's shoe-box diorama. "It's a tiny thing, bright, shabby, all felt and glue." Why should one little life matter? Isn't it all silly, inconsequential, hopelessly fragile? The novelist comments, "It isn't failure but it requires more of you, the whole effort does; just being present and grateful. . . ."

In whatever form it comes, the dragon shows us the fleeting beauty of everyday life. Alan says that he always tries to remember that the person he's talking to is going to die. "It's not as morbid as it sounds. When I remember that both I and the person I am talking to are going to die—especially if the other person is rich, powerful or influential—I find the conversation goes better. We share a common mortality. Exposing that secret helps drain away fear and posturing, and adds an element of expectancy and surprise."

True Hope and the Expectant Heart

The life of the soul is in great part an act of waiting, of living with a sense of expectancy and openness to the unexpected. The human heart cannot help but *expect*. Simone Weil writes, "At the bottom of every human being, from earliest infancy until the tomb, there is something that goes on indomitably expecting, in the teeth of all experience of crimes committed, suffered, and witnessed, that good and not evil will be done to him. It is that above all that is the sacred in every human being."

Novelist John Updike echoes this idea. While acknowledging the living hell of some people's lives, he notes that, "Wherever a church spire is raised, though dismal slums surround it and a dazed widow kneels under it, this Hell is opposed by a rumor of good news, by an irrational confirmation of the plenitude we feel is our birthright." Life may suck sometimes but we need to be open to the motions of grace. Out of the deadness of winter comes the promise of new life.

Simply waiting through winter requires a kind of courage. For some people it is an act of courage just to get up in the morning and face the day with hope. The movement from courage to hope is crucial but can seem nearly impossible when the spirit is frozen—when there's no movement, just a feeling of deadness. It's then that we're most challenged to trust the future. We nurse within us the seeds of hope—that there are places where the dormant heart can grow, and that the future holds the possibility of glorious surprise.

Let Go, Stay Open

One of winter's lessons is that spring cannot come if we insist always on being in control. We cannot retrieve or undo the past, and we don't have a handle on the future. As the compulsive Jack Nicholson character discovers in *As Good As It Gets,* a tight grip is lethal. He

cherished the illusion that he could avoid life's messier aspects by isolating himself from others, by literally never stepping on the cracks.

That we can somehow hold on to life is the most persistent illusion, even if we intellectually accept the fact of mortality. It's remarkable how often people are taken by surprise when that illusion finally
evaporates. Letting go can then become the ultimate occasion for gratitude, even for hilarious, liberating, soul-overflowing joy.

Here's a lesson from the Theravadan Buddhist meditation master
known as the Venerable Achaan Chah Subato:

> One day some people came and asked: "How can you be happy in a
> world of such impermanence, where you can't protect your loved
> ones from harm, illness and death?"
>
> The master held up a glass and said: "Someone gave me this
> glass, and I really like this glass. It holds my water admirably, and it
> glistens in the sunlight. I touch it and it rings! One day the wind may
> blow it off the shelf, or my elbow may knock it from the table.
>
> "I know this glass is already broken, so I enjoy it incredibly."

Perhaps it's a question of what kind of world you think you live in? Is it
one in which there's an answer—eventually—for everything? Or one
of ever-expanding mystery and exploration? The life of the soul means
a life of "expanding ambiguity," as Brian Mountford puts it, in which
the great sacred texts "expand rather than simplify." A lot of people
find this open view of life hard to take.

The Master of the Universe Is Dying

We have things to learn and choices to make about our death and
dying. Saint Francis of Assisi spoke of death as sister to be greeted
with quiet acceptance. Belden Lane writes about looking into the
tired and ancient eyes of the dragon, discerning a wisdom growing
slowly in himself and feeding on ordinariness.

For our friend Henry, dying was an epic journey from knowing
everything to knowing nothing, from self-love to true love, from isolation to communion. Watching Henry let go was painful. There he was,

in his late eighties, still trying to run the world from his hospital bed. You could see the confusion and frustration in his eyes. He was a kind of spiritual con man: he had fooled death all his life and now there it was, staring at him from the foot of the bed. He wasn't, after all, an exception. He was going to die just like everyone else.

Henry was a shrewd businessman, capable of being ruthless or sentimental as best served his needs. He had made a lot on money with what he called his "lucky strike." His business idol was Al "Chainsaw" Dunlap, who specialized in hostile takeovers and draining his acquisitions dry.

Henry's friends were few but his wives were many: four marriages produced five estranged children. His current wife, half his age, tried to love him but somehow did everything wrong. She dragged him to opera and symphony openings from which, angry and sleepy, he insisted on leaving early. Mainly, she couldn't perform the miracle of making him immortal. Henry's life in retirement was trips to the office "to keep his hand in" (and be a nuisance to his colleagues), rounds of golf, and lunches at his clubs. In short, he had "everything" and was terminally sour and unhappy.

Henry, however, became witness to his own diminishment. One day he collapsed over lunch, and suddenly he was in hospital with a badly damaged heart and a terrible prognosis. Tubes everywhere, and "those idiot" doctors not knowing what to do.

Henry's luck just then was in having one friend who saw through his bluster and bonhomie to the struggling human soul underneath. This was George, whom we met at the very start of this book: the old gent with advanced prostate cancer but the best attitude of anyone we know. George had known Henry since their college days—though since he'd fallen on hard times, he hadn't heard much from his old buddy.

"He wasn't always like this," George recalled. "In college, we were inseparable, and everyone wanted to be with us. We hardly went to class and had a ball. I'm amazed we graduated. Henry was always driven, though. His dad worked for the phone company and Henry was determined not to follow in his father's footsteps. And he made it. But no matter how successful he got, it was never quite enough."

When George learned about Henry's heart attack, he sent him, for old times' sake, a card depicting their alma mater. His note read, "Henry, what times we had! I love you. I know you're having a rough time. As they say in the old melodramas, Come home! All is forgiven."

Henry was puzzled by this at first, then a little annoyed. Then he burst out laughing and, before he knew it, had begun to cry. A place in his heart suddenly gaped wide. It was a place of great pain compounded of regret and shame. His wife, Janet, was in his room when the breakthrough came. He let the tears flow, and the pain gradually gave way to acceptance of what was happening to him, and gratitude for the love of his wife and George. "I've been a fool," he told her. "I love you so much."

Henry and Janet had three months after that, a remarkable time for them and anyone who saw them then. He talked and talked, at least while he had strength enough, seemingly wanting to make up for all the time he'd never really conversed but only barked orders. Later, he did a lot of listening, smiling gently as Janet read to him, relayed ordinary news, or assured him of her love. Henry died at home, holding George's card in one hand and Janet's hand in the other.

Leadership expert Tracy Goss, in *The Last Word on Power,* suggests that we accept—as if accepting a gift—these facts:

- Life does not turn out the way it "should"
- Nor does life turn out the way it "shouldn't"
- Life turns out the way it "does"

Henry had believed he could create a perfect world, or that one existed if only he could find it. In his hospital bed, he began learning to free himself from the illusion that he could control life, that life could turn out the way it "should." His last gift was learning to be thankful that he wasn't in control! He began to accept that life turns out the way it does. This is as good as it gets.

He had always longed for a wholeness he couldn't understand. This deep longing makes people vulnerable to their aching desires—especially those who land at the top of the heap of human arrangements. Henry found El Dorado in Silicon Valley, and had to let it all go in a solitary hospital bed. But he died with real treasure in each hand: the love of a friend and the love of a wife who, until that time, didn't know how to love him. His winter unexpectedly turned to spring. The manner of Henry's dying turned out to be a great gift to all who were able to see him in those last few months.

As W. H. Auden wrote in a poem to his godson, "Thank God your being is unnecessary"—which is a way of saying, "Thank God you're not God!" Enormous grace is found in accepting as a gift whatever life gives. Henry gave up being his own divinity—what a relief. And it was worth it. Love is worth it, even if only for a couple of months. Believing it should be otherwise is a waste of time.

Preview Your Death

Facing one's actual dying can be a great teacher. It can break through a lifetime's worth of resistance to living gratefully. Literature is full of stories like Henry's: Dickens characters who reform on their death-beds or, like Scrooge, through supernatural experiences that resemble a kind of death. But how much better would their lives—and all the lives around them—have been if they could have found a way to live fully into their mortality! Dickens, at least, took care to provide clear models of contrasting characters, like Scrooge's nephew Fred, who, to use our phrase, have gone live and live in gratitude.

Rarely, someone is privileged to come back from a near-death experience with a new view of life. The philosopher A. J. (Freddie) Ayer made his name when quite young with his classic book *Language, Truth and Logic*. Ayer insisted on seeing everything through the filter of "scientific verification." A year before his death in 1989, he choked on a piece of smoked salmon smuggled into his hospital room by a former mistress and was clinically dead for four minutes. He revived to report that he had been pulled toward a red light. "I saw a Divine Being," he said. "I'm afraid I'm going to have to revise all my various books and opinions." He didn't get around to revising his books, but his wife reports, "Freddie became so much nicer after he died. He was not nearly so boastful. He took an interest in other people."

Students of ancient religious literature were advised to practice "mortification." The idea was to get much of dying over with before one's actual death—not to be morbid but to allow life to flow in ways that really mattered. It was a way of transforming the great dragon of death. The novelist Walker Percy wrote somewhere that the truly spiritually alive person is an ex-suicide. He or she has faced the possibility of not existing and decided to live. He goes to work with a light heart because he doesn't have to.

The Need to Praise

Another element to come out of our hoping and waiting for death is the discovery in us of a voice to give praise—to say "thank you!" The ability to praise may be the most crucial gift: a natural response to our astonishment at the goodness of existence. When the grateful impulse arises, human life begins to sparkle, even in the darkness of the soul's winter. Gratitude brings the rumor of good news, the hint that spring is on the way.

The philosopher, scientist, and priest Teilhard de Chardin said, "Humanity is being taken to the point where it will have to choose between suicide and adoration." What can this mean? A choice between a dying life and a living death? A choice between going live and playing dead? Between saying yes and no? The slow suicide of self-absorption, or turning outwards in gratitude and adoration when we see, in the light of our mortality, that every moment is a gift?

Gratitude Practice: Write Your Own Obituary

Charles Handy, in *The Age of Unreason*, suggests that we practice writing our own obituary, as if it were being written by a good friend. Don't write more than 200 words. This isn't easy because it requires you to envisage your death as a real event. Doing this can be a great release, however, because it allows you to think in more concrete terms about living fully in the time you have. The exercise forces you to stand at the end of your life and look back. From that perspective, what does what you're doing now look like? How would you reshape your life based on how you would like to be remembered?

Alan tried writing his obituary and came up with this:

Alan Jones died last Tuesday in his home on the Santa Barbara coast. He would have been 84 next month. His wife of 25 years was with him, as were his children and three of his seven grandchildren. He was working on his twentieth book, *The Cunning of God* (about interreligious dialogue and experience). He and his wife were well-known for their hospitality to young people and others who enjoyed good conversation. Dr. Jones founded the Institute for New Politics in 2007, which is now part of U.C. Santa Barbara, and was responsible for new and successful experiments in health care and education. He often expressed impatience with the contemporary Church, which was neither liberal nor traditional enough for his tastes. His faith was always shared with a sense of humor and sometimes with a strong sense of irony. Last rites were administered by his long-time friend, Father François Legaux, former dean of Chartres. He states in his will that his most important legacy is the collection of love poems he wrote for his wife intermittently over the course of their marriage. The will concludes with words written by Charles Williams at the end of his letters, "Under the mercy. . . ."

If you do the exercise, be sure to show the result to an honest friend for a reality check.

The Cycle of Dying and Rising

The turning of the seasons gives form to our genetic predisposition to unreasonable hope. The writer Lewis Smedes tells of a springtime experience after a close encounter with death, when his medical odds of surviving were twenty to one. He writes of a moment in his hospital bed when he felt what he calls *the almost unbearable goodness of being alive:*

> It was then that I learned that gratitude is the best feeling I would ever have, the ultimate joy of living. It was better than sex, better than winning the lottery, better than watching your daughter graduate from college, better and deeper than any other feeling. It is perhaps the genesis of all other really good feelings in the human repertoire. I am sure that nothing in life can ever match the feeling of being held by a gracious energy percolating from the abyss where beats the loving heart of God.

In Norse mythology, there's a mythical tree of which one side is dead and the other living. It's our task to circle the trunk, climbing first on the living side and then on the dead, and so on until we reach the top. All cultures have such stories of cyclical dying and rising.

The mystics would tell us to give thanks for it all—the diminishments as well as the fulfillments. The news of Alan's cancer pushed him onto the dead side of the tree; little did he know that if he kept moving, he would soon be back on the living side.

The Catholic writer Leon Bloy observes that "there are places in the heart that do not yet exist!" If our hearts are open, there will be unimaginable surprises. Life's obstructions, failures and disappointments have much to teach us about the cycle of gratitude. Knowing we are lost is often the way we begin a new journey.

Holy Compassion

Is there a way of accepting it all joyfully—even the deformities and betrayals that cause us pain and despair? Can we view ourselves and others, defects and all, with "a holy compassion"? This can be an arduous but life-giving discipline. The elements of a life lived in gratitude begin to appear: wakefulness, astonishment, compassion, service, moral direction, joy, praise.

The recent memoir about novelist Iris Murdoch by her husband, John Bayley, and the film based on it were moving reminders of what it takes to be present and grateful in the winter of our lives. Murdoch, an elegant stylist and philosopher, suffered terrible diminishment from Alzheimer's, and in the end lost control of everything, becoming fearful, unkempt, and eccentric.

Long before Alzheimer's struck, she wrote that we are called to lead lives of virtue and of kindness, because that's all there is. Underneath is the rubble of our own inventions, the debris of contingency. Everything gives way, in the end, to the god of time. Murdoch not only lost her vital ability to think clearly, to remember, and to communicate, but she also suffered greatly from her fear of other people, her habit of collecting rubbish, and her refusal to change her clothes at bedtime. According to her husband, however, she took on Christlike qualities of tolerance, amusement, and good nature. So who was she in the end? Was she reducible to the smelly creature who collected rubbish?

The truth is that she was loved and lovable. This cannot be *proved*. All we can do is accept the invitation to see the world clearly as both beautiful and terrible. When we see both clearly, the only appropriate response is gratitude. Even outrage—the good and reasonable kind— is born of gratitude. First we see the wonder of the world, then we are often saddened or enraged by the mess we make of things. Yet in the depths of the mess and muddle of being human, there is still the invitation to radical amazement.

Seeing Clearly and Choosing Gratitude

In an essay, Murdoch describes an incident when she is looking out her window, "in an anxious and resentful state of mind, brooding perhaps on some damage to my prestige. Then suddenly I observe a hovering kestrel. In a moment everything is altered. There is nothing but kestrel. And when I return to thinking of the other matter it seems less important." In an act of self-forgetfulness another, larger truth emerges.

We call this self-forgetfulness *contemplation*—the act of seeing what appears to be "the sheer alien pointless independent existence of animals birds, stones, and trees." This self-forgetfulness isn't self-annihilation. Rather, it's is a form of pleasure, and indeed, of love: "Love is the extremely difficult realization that something other than oneself is real," Murdoch continues. And we have to move though all the seasons of grace to learn that lesson.

There is sadness too. We cannot ignore it. Reviewing our past, we are sometimes haunted by waste and failure. But practicing gratitude can help us come to terms with the landscape of our lives as it is, and to accept it with tenderness and blessing. Saying "thank you!" helps set the bits and pieces of life in the right order. "All losses are restor'd and sorrows end," as Shakespeare's Puck reassures us.

Just giving thanks will not magically relieve us of being haunted by past failures, but we do have a choice. We can choose resentment or something else—rage, humor, sorrow, acceptance? And as long as we don't get stuck in any one stage, we can find a place where gratitude is possible.

As Good as It Gets

The mess? The tragic and cruel along with the glory and longing, the fools' gold and the true? The winter of the soul? This is as good as it gets. Believing this isn't being passive or fatalistic. In appreciating the goodness of existence, we find ourselves on the side of justice and mercy.

True goodness—pizza and beer for dinner when you're hungry, a hot bath when you're tired, a great day hike, or holding your kids—expands and flourishes when we wake up to the wonder of being alive. When we make that leap, we move from sighing "This is as good as it gets" with resignation or cynicism, to proclaiming it with expectancy and hope.

The life of the soul is the greatest comedy and drama of all. We struggle to say "yes" to life, accept it as gift, knowing we pass this way but once. We live as courageously as we know how, since we are not in control of the unknown and unexpected. We embrace hope as a way of living into the thanks we struggle to say every day. The new really is possible. We expect it. We work for it. We fail. We succeed and fail again.

In short, we gain the glory of being human by accepting our place in a family of actors in a moral adventure—blessing what is real, astonished at the wonder of being alive. It doesn't get any better.

Bibliography and Recommended Reading

Ackerman, Diane. *Deep Play.* New York: Random House, 1999. ISBN 0679771352

Anderson, Hans Christian. *The Snow Queen.* New York: Anchor, 1983. ISBN 0385189516

Armstrong, Karen. Introduction from *Every Eye Beholds You* by Thomas J. Craughwell. Orlando, Florida: Harcourt Brace & Co., 1999. ISBN 0151004838

Auden, W. H. *Collected Poems.* Edward Mendelson, editor. New York: Vintage Books, 1991. ISBN 0679731970

Bayley, John. *Elegy for Iris.* New York: St. Martin's Press, 2001. ISBN 0312421117

Beckett, Samuel. *Three Novels by Samuel Beckett: Molloy, Malone Dies, the Unnamable.* Cambridge, England: Grove Press, 1995. ISBN 0802150918

Beckett, Samuel. *Waiting for Godot.* Cambridge, England: Grove Press, 1997. ISBN 0802130348

Burnett, Frances Hodgson. *The Secret Garden.* New York: Harper Collins Juvenile Books, 1987. ISBN 0397321651

Carse, James P. *Finite and Infinite Games.* New York: Ballentine, 1994. ISBN 0345341848

Carse, James P. *Breakfast at the Victory: The Mysticism of Ordinary Experience.* San Francisco: Harper San Francisco, 1995. ISBN 0062511718

Carson, Rachael. *The Sense of Wonder.* New York: Harper Collins, 1998. ISBN 006757520X

Carson, Rachel. *Silent Spring.* Boston: Mariner Books, Houghton-Mifflin: 1994. ISBN 0395683297

Chodron, Pema. *When Things Fall Apart: Heart Advice for Difficult Times.* Boston: Shambala, 1997. ISBN 157062160

Corn, Charles Philip. *Distant Islands: Travels Across Indonesia.* New York: Viking Press, 1991. ISBN 0670823740

Chatwin, Bruce. *The Songlines.* New York: Penguin USA, 1988. ISBN 0140094296

Cunningham, Michael. *The Hours.* London: Picador, Pan Macmillan, 2000. ISBN 0312243022

Frankl, Victor. *Man's Search for Meaning.* New York: Washington Square Press, 1997. ISBN 0671023373

Gregory of Nyssa. *The Life of Moses.* Abraham J. Malherbe, translator; Everett Ferguson, translator. Baltimore: Paulist Press, 1979. ISBN 080912123

Hanh, Thich Nhat. *Jesus and Buddha as Brothers.* New York: Riverhead, 2000. ISBN 1573228303

Hanh, Thich Nhat. *Living Buddha, Living Christ.* With David Steindl-Rast. New York: Riverhead, 1997. ISBN 1573228303

Handy, Charles. *The Age of Unreason.* Boston: Harvard Business School Press, 1998. ISBN 0875843018

Johnston, Tracy. *Shooting the Boh: A Woman's Voyage Down the Wildest River in Borneo.* Vintage: New York, 1992. ISBN 0679740104

Lane, Belden C. *The Solace of Fierce Landscapes: Exploring Desert and Mountain Spirituality.* Oxford, England: Oxford University Press, 1998. ISBN 0195116828

Lonergan, Father Bernard. *Method in Theology.* University of Toronto Press, 1990. ISBN 080206809X

Mayle, Peter. *A Year In Provence.* New York: Vintage, 1991. ISBN 0679731148

McCullough, David. *John Adams.* New York: Simon & Schuster, 2001. ISBN 0684813637

McLennan, Scotty. *Finding Your Religion: When the Faith You Grew Up With Has Lost Its Meaning.* Harper San Francisco, 2000. ISBN 0060653469

Nussbaum, Martha. *Poetic Justice.* Boston: Beacon Press, 1995. ISBN 0807041092

Oldenburg, Roy. *The Great Good Place: Cafes, Coffee Shops, Bookstores, Bars, Hair Salons, and Other Hangouts at the Heart of a Community.* New York: Marlowe & Co., Avalon, 1999. ISBN 1569246815

Oliver, Mary. *Dream Work.* New York: Atlantic Monthly Press, 1986. ISBN 0871130696

Peck, M. Scott. *In Search of Stones; A Pilgrimage of Faith, Reason and Discovery.* Santa Ana, California: Books on Tape, Inc., 1997. ISBN 0913369632

Rabelais, François. *Gargantua and Pantagruel.* New York: Knopf, Everyman's Library, 1994. ISBN 0679431373

Radcliffe, Timothy. *I Call You Friends.* New York: Continuum, 2001. ISBN 0826451888

Rattigan, Terence. *Separate Tables.* London, England: Methuen. ISBN 1854594249

Rilke, Maria Ranier. *Letters to a Young Poet.* Stephen Mitchell, translator. New York: Random House (Modern Library), 2001. ISBN 0679642323

Rilke, Maria Ranier. *Selected Poems.* Robert Bly, translation and commentary. New York: HarperCollins, 1981. ISBN 0060907274

Smedes, Lewis. *Quoted in Context: Martin E. Marty on Religion and Culture.* June 15, 2000.

Thoreau, Henry David. *The Maine Woods.* New York: Penguin USA, 1988. ISBN 0140170138

Tyler, Anne. *Dinner at the Homesick Restaurant.* New York: Ballentine Books, 1996. ISBN 0449911594

Tolkien, J.R.R. *The Hobbit and The Lord of the Rings.* Boston: Mariner Books, Houghton-Mifflin, 1999. ISBN 0618002251

Walsh, Roger. *Essential Spirituality: The Seven Central Practices to Awaken Heart and Mind.* Hoboken, New Jersey: John Wiley & Sons, 2000. ISBN 0471392161

White, T.H. *The Once and Future King.* New York: Ace Books, Penguin Putnam, 1987. ISBN 0441627404

Whitman, Walt. *Leaves of Grass.* New York: Metro Books, 2001. ISBN 1586632108

Wilde, Oscar. *The Importance of Being Earnest.* Alexandria, Virginia: Orchises Press, 1990. ISBN 0914061119

Winterson, Jeannette. *Written on the Body.* New York: Vintage Books, 1994. ISBN 0679744479

Whyte, David. *The Heart Aroused: Poetry and the Preservation of the Soul in Corporate America.* Forthcoming: Currency/Doubleday, (October 29, 2002). ISBN 0385484186

Whyte, David. *Crossing the Unknown Sea: Work as a Pilgrimage of Identity.* New York: Riverhead Books, 2002. ISBN 1573229148

Index